D1627134

ACCOMPLISHING THE *Impossible*

ACCOMPLISHING THE *Impossible*

WHAT GOD DOES
WHAT WE CAN DO

RUSSELL M. NELSON

SALT LAKE CITY, UTAH

Image credits:
Shutterstock/© somchaij, page vi; © Jerry Sanchez, pages 13, 53, 105, and 139; © THPStock, pages 14–15, and 66–67; © Standret, page 16; © Galyna Andrushko, pages 26, 84, 92, 106, and 118; © Xuanlu Wang, page 36; © Andrey tiyk, page 44; © Dariush M, page 54; © mythja, page 68; © Creative Travel Projects, page 76; © melis, page 132; © Paul Aniszewski, page 140; © komkrit Preechachanwate, background.

Visit us at DeseretBook.com

Library of Congress Cataloging-in-Publication Data

Nelson, Russell Marion, author.

Accomplishing the impossible : what God does, what we can do / Russell M. Nelson.

pages cm

Includes bibliographical references and index.

ISBN 978-1-62972-125-5 (hardbound : alk. paper)

1. Spiritual life—The Church of Jesus Christ of Latter-day Saints. 2. Christian life—Mormon authors. 3. The Church of Jesus Christ of Latter-day Saints—Doctrines. 4. Mormon Church—Doctrines. I. Title.

BX8656.N43 2015

248.4'89332—dc23 2015024185

Printed in the United States of America
Publishers Printing, Salt Lake City, UT

10 9 8 7 6 5 4 3 2

CONTENTS

The Lord has more in mind for you

than you have in mind for yourself!

As you love Him and keep His commandments,

great rewards—

EVEN UNIMAGINABLE ACHIEVEMENTS—

may be yours.

INTRODUCTION

ACCOMPLISHING THE IMPOSSIBLE

Many years ago, I was teaching a missionary discussion to a woman from Great Britain. I was teaching about the Lord Jesus Christ and how He had restored His gospel through the Prophet Joseph Smith. She really liked the teachings of the gospel, but she had a hard time accepting the Prophet's First Vision. She said she could believe in the Restoration more sincerely if God the Father and His Son Jesus Christ had appeared to the Archbishop of Canterbury!

Actually, the fact that the Father and the Son appeared to an untitled youth is one of the most remarkable aspects of the Restoration. Joseph Smith did not have to "unlearn" anything. He was tutored personally by Them. Joseph was also tutored by other heavenly messengers, including Moroni, John the Baptist, Peter, James, John, Moses, Elias, and Elijah.[1] Joseph's mission in mortality was foreordained.

His receptive and pristine mind was open to the Lord's instruction. But, by worldly standards, Joseph was most unlikely. And his task to be the Prophet of this last dispensation seemed totally impossible. This example demonstrates a principle that is often true of how the Lord works: He uses the unlikely to accomplish the impossible!

This pattern is one the Lord has used repeatedly throughout history. For instance, you know the story of David who slew Goliath with a stone and a sling.[2] That was another example of how the Lord uses the unlikely to accomplish the impossible.

You may remember the account of Gideon, as recorded in the book of Judges. In his capacity as a servant of the Lord, Gideon was preparing to lead his forces against the Midianite enemies when "the Lord said unto Gideon, The people that are with thee are too many, . . . lest Israel vaunt themselves . . . saying, Mine own hand hath saved me."

So the Lord told Gideon to excuse all who were afraid. That trimmed the number from 22,000 down to 10,000. Then the Lord said unto Gideon, "The people are yet too many." So He ordered a drink test. They went down to the water. Some bowed down upon their knees to drink. Others cupped their hands to their mouths to drink.

The Lord said unto Gideon, "By the three hundred men

that lapped will I save you, and deliver the Midianites into thine hand."[3]

The Lord delivered the victory to Gideon and his men. They were outnumbered about 500 to 1.[4] Here again we see the pattern: the Lord uses the unlikely to accomplish the impossible.

Think of Moses. In his advanced years, he was called to lead the children of Israel out of bondage in Egypt.[5] You know what happened. Moses stretched out his hand over the Red Sea; and the Lord caused the sea to be divided. And the children of Israel walked across on the ground.[6]

Think of Joshua. He led the children of Israel across the River Jordan at flood time. In faith, they walked to that swollen river with priests in front carrying the ark of the covenant, and when the soles of those priests' feet were wet, the waters of the Jordan were heaped up, allowing the faithful to pass along to the promised land.[7] For those Israelites who followed Moses and Joshua, deep water was divinely divided to allow the faithful to reach their appointed destination. Again we see the pattern: the Lord uses the unlikely to accomplish the impossible.

Jumping ahead to the nineteenth century, we see the pattern emerge once again. Have you ever wondered why the Master waited so long to inaugurate the promised "restitution of all things"?[8] Any competitor knows the disadvantage of allowing an opponent to get too far ahead. Suppose for a moment you are a member of a team. The coach calls you by name and says: "It is time for you to enter the game. But the going will be mighty tough. The score at this moment is one billion, one hundred forty-three million to six, and your team is the one with the six points!"[9]

That large number, 1,143,000,000, was the approximate population of the earth in the year 1830, when the restored Church of Jesus Christ was officially organized with six members.[10] The location was in a rural part of New York state. With this little handful of people, the Lord's work was begun. Think of the enormity of their assignment! It included the following:

- The gospel was to be preached to every kindred, nation, tongue, and people.
- Ordinary human beings were to become Saints.
- Redemptive temple work was to be done for all who had ever lived.

Yes, with that assignment, the promised dispensation of the latter days had commenced, and they were the ones to usher it forth!

If any tasks ever deserved the label "impossible," these massive assignments all qualified! But the early Saints knew this biblical truth: "With men this is impossible; but with God all things are possible."[11]

So much for history. Now we are living in the twenty-first century. Might these patterns apply to us? Scripture describes us and what we may experience as Latter-day Saints. "God hath chosen the foolish things of the world to confound the wise; and God hath chosen the weak things of the world to confound the . . . mighty."[12]

Those "weak ones" even include us—the Brethren. For example, in 1984, in a most unexpected way, Elder Dallin H. Oaks and I were called away from our professions of law and medicine, respectively, to serve as Apostles of the Lord. In the following year, President Ezra Taft Benson gave to me the assignment to supervise the work of the Lord in Europe and Africa, with a specific charge to open the nations of Eastern Europe then under the yoke of communism. (This assignment remained with me until 1990, when it was rotated to Elder Dallin H. Oaks.)

If ever a task seemed impossible to me, that was it. In the ensuing years, I tried my best. In each atheistic nation, I was never wanted and never welcome. Their governmental leaders wouldn't even give appointments to a man who professed faith in God. In fact, at that time, some believers were imprisoned or even executed.

Those countries kept good records on visits by foreigners.

I was on record as an American heart surgeon who, as a volunteer, had previously taught in some of those countries. Paired with Elder Hans B. Ringger of the Seventy, a Swiss engineer and architect, our partnership was disarming to them. We were truly unlikely, and different from leaders of other faith groups. Country by country, we labored diligently in Russia, Ukraine, Romania, Bulgaria, Belarus, Czechoslovakia, Hungary, Yugoslavia, Estonia, Poland, Armenia, and the German Democratic Republic. Each country presented different challenges for us. We did the very best we could, and then the Lord made up the difference. He did what we could not do. Following are just a few of the many miracles we experienced.

Upon authorization from the First Presidency, I was privileged to dedicate the land of Hungary for the establishment of the gospel on Easter Sunday, April 19, 1987. Two days later, Elder Ringger and I met with the chairman of the Council of Religious Affairs, Imré Miklos. Our reception at first was a bit tense. It was clear that we were neither welcome nor wanted. Things were not going particularly well. But then I felt impressed to let this leader know that two days prior to this meeting, I had offered a special apostolic prayer for his country and for its people. As this was mentioned, his countenance changed. Now he was listening. A meeting planned for thirty minutes lasted an hour and a half.

From that point forward, he became our friend and advocate. Several subsequent meetings were successfully held. Fourteen months later, on June 14, 1988, Elder Ringger and I returned to Budapest for formal ceremonies with Mr. Miklos that confirmed official recognition for the Church in Hungary.

Bulgaria was another country that posed particular challenges to us. When Elder Ringger and I first arrived in Sofia, Bulgaria, on October 30, 1988, we had been led to believe, through our indirect third-party contact, that we would be met at the airport and that proper appointments had been made. (Incidentally, it had been our experience that most leaders in these totalitarian governments did *not* confirm any arrangements in writing.) So we went to Bulgaria in faith. We arrived late at night. No one was there to greet us. We took a taxi, which delivered us to the wrong hotel. Once we made that discovery, we trudged, luggage in hand, through a snowstorm until we finally found our correct accommodations. Our frustration continued the next day as bilingual telephone operators at the hotel were not able to help us identify either the office or the leaders with whom we needed to meet. We were at a complete dead end. All we could do was to pray for help.

Our prayers were answered. In a marvelous way, a day later, at 10:00 a.m., we met with Mr. Tsviatko Tsvetkov, head of the religious affairs department for the country. He had just returned to the city, and his interpreter was available also. Incredible!

At first, the atmosphere was pretty cold. He didn't know we were coming. Through his interpreter, he scolded, "Nelson? Ringger? Mormons? I've never heard of you."

I replied, "That makes us even. We have never heard of you, either. It's time we got acquainted." Everyone laughed, and we went on to have a great meeting.

Elder Ringger and I returned to Sofia in February 1990, at which time, as authorized by the First Presidency, an apostolic dedicatory prayer was given on February 13 at Park Na Svobodata, which means "Liberty Park." A new mission was created on July 1, 1991. Official recognition for the Church was granted by the Bulgarian government on July 10, 1991.

The conversion of the pioneer members of the Church in Russia is another story of miracles. At that time, recognition of a church in the U.S.S.R. was not given on a federal basis but was granted locally. A petition was required from a minimum of twenty adult members of the Church, all Soviet citizens residing in a given political district. Open preaching of the gospel was not allowed because that was deemed to be an infringement on the rights of others who chose not to believe in any religion. Thus, we were left with a real dilemma. Without missionaries, how could we get a congregation of twenty members in any district? And how could we teach the gospel without first having twenty members so that we could obtain legal recognition?

But the Lord works in marvelous ways. Our branch president and his wife found the Church and were baptized on July 1, 1989, while in Budapest, Hungary. Russian-speaking home teachers from Helsinki, Finland, were assigned to visit these new converts upon their return to Leningrad.

Another woman who had temporarily left Leningrad found the Church in a miraculous manner. This beautiful young mother, Svetlana, had importuned the Lord in prayer to make it possible for her to obtain a Bible written in the Russian language. Such a Bible was rare, precious, and very expensive. In the fall of 1989, with her husband's encouragement, she went to Helsinki with their young child in quest for a Bible. While walking through a park in Helsinki, she stepped upon an object hidden beneath the ground cover of autumn leaves. She picked it up and found it to be the answer to her prayers. It was a Bible written in the Russian language. So excited was she that she joyfully recounted the story of this great discovery to another mother who was also in the park with her youngster. The second mother then replied to Svetlana, "Would you like to have *another* book about Jesus Christ, also written in the Russian language?" Svetlana, of course, answered in the affirmative. The other mother then provided Svetlana with a Russian copy of the Book of Mormon and invited her to church. This other mother was Raija Kemppainen, wife of Jussi Kemppainen, then president of the Baltic District of the Finland Helsinki Mission. Shortly thereafter, Svetlana joined The Church of Jesus Christ of Latter-day Saints, having returned with her child to Leningrad.

These early converts invited choice friends into their homes to hear news of the restored gospel of Jesus Christ, and many of these gratefully responded to the gospel message and were baptized.

On April 26, 1990, we met with governmental officials and subsequently submitted application papers for recognition of the Leningrad Branch. That very day, I offered a prayer of gratitude and rededication in the Summer Gardens adjacent to the Neva River, just beyond Mars Field, where Elder Francis M. Lyman of the Quorum of the Twelve had dedicated Russia for the preaching of the gospel on August 6, 1903.

Our request for formal recognition for our branch in Leningrad was granted on September 13, 1990. Thus, an important precedent was established that congregations in other cities would follow. The Church of Jesus Christ of Latter-day Saints was given official recognition by the Republic of Russia on May 28, 1991. This historic decision was announced in Moscow one month later by the vice president of the republic, Alexander Rutskoi.

Gratefully, before President Ezra Taft Benson passed away, Elder Oaks and I were able to report that the Church was now established in all countries of Eastern Europe!

I testify to you that the Lord meant what He said when He declared: "I will show unto the children of men that I am able to do mine own work."[13] Yes, I am an eyewitness. I am a part of that pattern: the Lord used the unlikely to accomplish the impossible.

Now, let us apply this pattern to you. You will have moments of dismay. But you should remember that you are literally and truly a son or daughter of Almighty God. You have been created in His very image.

Physically, He wants you to honor the body He has given you. He wants you to treasure and care for your body as your own personal temple.

Spiritually, He has sent you here to be successful and to have joy in your journey in mortality. He wants you to know that "with God nothing shall be impossible."[14] You are entitled through your worthiness to receive revelation to help you with your righteous endeavors. You may take upon you the name of the Lord. You may pray in His holy name. You can qualify to speak in the sacred name of God.[15] It matters not that times of tribulation will come. Your prayerful access to help is just as real as it was when David battled his Goliath.

As a Latter-day Saint, you too can accomplish the impossible. You can help shape the destiny of the entire human family! You and your fellow Saints will be scattered like seeds in the wind to build up the Church in all parts of the world. As you know and apply the teachings of the Lord in your life and in your work, you can change the world. You will become a precious part of His perennial pattern: the Lord uses the unlikely to accomplish the impossible!

WHAT GOD DOES

Do we believe in angels?

WE BELIEVE IN ANGELS—

heavenly messengers—seen and unseen;

AND EARTHLY ANGELS

who know whom to help and how to help.

CHAPTER 1

HE SENDS ANGELS

In preparation for the rededication of the newly remodeled Ogden Temple, my family and I attended an open house tour of that beautiful building. Among the many paintings and murals in the Ogden Temple, one especially caught my attention. It is drenched in doctrine. Painted by Robert Shepherd, it is a large mural located on the main floor in the center of the temple. It is an artistic portrayal of the Lord Jesus Christ, with Moses and Elias on each side of the Savior, standing atop the Mount of Transfiguration. There they conferred keys of the priesthood upon Peter, James, and John.[1]

As I admired that elegant work of art, I explained to my family that it was that same Peter, James, and John, who thus received keys of the priesthood, that appeared to the Prophet Joseph Smith and Oliver Cowdery in 1829, to restore the Melchizedek Priesthood in this dispensation.[2] Before that, on May 15, 1829,[3] under the direction of Peter, James, and John, the Aaronic Priesthood had been conferred upon Joseph Smith and Oliver Cowdery by John the Baptist.

In the evening, at the end of our tour of the Ogden Temple, our family enjoyed a view as we departed. I asked the children: What is that golden figure standing atop the spire of the temple? Who does that represent? Almost in unison, they replied, "The angel Moroni!"

I was pleased. They knew his name. Moroni, the last in a line of prophets in an ancient American civilization, held priesthood keys for an ancient, sacred record that we now know as the Book of Mormon.[4] Moroni was foreordained for that responsibility. That was revealed in the biblical book of Revelation. There John prophesied: "I saw another angel fly in the midst of heaven, having the everlasting gospel to preach unto them that dwell on the earth, and to every nation, and kindred, and tongue, and people."[5]

As we remember the angel Moroni, we might ask, are there other angels? Do we really believe in angels? Well, the answer is *no* and *yes*. *No,* we do not believe in angels as most people imagine them, with colossal wings and cherubic faces. But we do believe in angels who serve as appointed messengers from heaven.

The word *angel* is very meaningful. It comes to us from the Greek language. The Greek word, ΑΓΓΕΛΟΣ, means "messenger."[6] This same noun is centered in the Greek word for *gospel,* which is ΕΥΑΓΓΕΛΙΟΝ. Its literal meaning is "good message" or "good news," with an implication of a heavenly or angelic source. ΕΥΑΓΓΕΛΙΟΝ is the very first word in the Greek New Testament ("*Gospel* According to St. Matthew").

At Christmastime, we speak of angels when we review the sweet story about shepherds who were tending their flocks by night: "And the angel [of the Lord] said unto them, Fear not: for, behold, I bring you good tidings of great joy, which shall be to all people.

"For unto you is born this day in the city of David a Saviour, which is Christ the Lord."[7]

The King James translators used five words, "I bring you good tidings," to express in English the meaning of a single word in the Greek text. That one Greek word is ΕΥΑΓΓΕΛΙΖΟ, which literally means "I announce good news." That good news is the gospel. That good news is Jesus Christ! He has come into the world. Notice in the center of the word ΕΥΑΓΓΕΛΙΖΟ is the root, ΑΓΓΕΛ, from the Greek word, ΑΓΓΕΛΟΣ, for heavenly messenger, or angel.

Do we believe in angels—heavenly messengers? Absolutely. Those shepherds knew. Angels provided comforting reassurance to them.

Now, in these latter days, we rejoice in the Restoration of the gospel. Many heavenly messengers, including angels, have participated. They have been a key part of accomplishing what may have seemed impossible in the eyes of the world.

Leading the way for those heavenly messengers were God the Father and Jesus Christ, who commenced the work of the Restoration in the year 1820 when They appeared to the fourteen-year-old Joseph Smith. Our Heavenly Father opened this dispensation with this stunning seven-word introduction: *"This is My Beloved Son. Hear Him!"*[8]

That visitation was the first of many appearances of Deity to the young prophet. Other visits included one in Hiram, Ohio, on February 16, 1832. Then Joseph Smith and Sidney Rigdon "beheld the glory of the Son, on the right hand of the Father."[9] Joseph recorded this description:

"We beheld the glory of the Son, on the right hand of the Father, and received of his fulness;

"And saw the holy angels, and them who are sanctified before his throne, worshiping God, and the Lamb, who worship him forever and ever.

"And now, after the many testimonies which have been given of him, this is the testimony, last of all, which we give of him: That he lives!

"For we saw him, even on the right hand of God; and we heard the voice bearing record that he is the Only Begotten of the Father."[10]

Another visitation came to the Prophet Joseph Smith in Kirtland, Ohio, on January 21, 1836, when he saw "the blazing throne of God, whereon was seated the Father and the Son."[11] Then Joseph learned that "the Lord, will judge all men according to their works, [and] according to the desire of their hearts."[12] He was also taught "that all children who die before they arrive at the years of accountability are saved in the celestial kingdom of heaven."[13]

Less than three months later, on April 3, 1836, heavenly messengers again came to the Prophet Joseph Smith. Oliver Cowdery was a witness. There the Lord Jehovah appeared in glory and accepted the newly dedicated Kirtland Temple as His holy house. Joseph recorded this eyewitness account:

"We saw the Lord standing upon the breastwork of the pulpit, before us; . . .

"His eyes were as a flame of fire; the hair of his head was white like the pure snow; his countenance shone above the brightness of the sun; and his voice was as the sound of the rushing of great waters, even the voice of Jehovah, saying:

"I am the first and the last; I am he who liveth, I am he who was slain; I am your advocate with the Father."[14]

Then, under the direction of the Lord, other heavenly messengers came. "Moses appeared . . . and committed . . . the keys of the gathering of Israel from the four parts of the earth."[15]

"After this, Elias appeared, and committed the dispensation of the gospel of Abraham, saying that in us and our seed all generations after us should be blessed."[16] Thus, an everlasting covenant was restored, as originally given to Abraham,[17] Isaac,[18] and Jacob,[19] more than four thousand years ago.

Then, "Elijah the prophet, who was taken to heaven without tasting death, stood before [them], and said:

"Behold, the time has fully come, which was spoken of by the mouth of Malachi—testifying that he [Elijah] should be sent, before the great and dreadful day of the Lord come—

"To turn the hearts of the fathers to the children, and the children to the fathers, lest the whole earth be smitten with a curse."[20]

This revelation from Elijah fulfilled a promise planted in Joseph's mind thirteen years earlier by the angel Moroni, on September 21, 1823.[21]

To me, it is interesting to note that in that instructive visit, Moroni referred to teachings of the Old Testament prophet Malachi. Moroni quoted from the book of Malachi.[22] In the Hebrew language of the Old Testament, the word *malachi* literally means "my messenger."[23] (*Malak* means "messenger," and the added *-i* indicates a possessive form.)

Other angels—heavenly messengers—have participated in the Restoration. And now we know more about them. Michael is identified as the archangel,[24] or chief angel.

Latter-day revelation informs us that Michael is Adam, patriarch of the human family.[25]

The angel Gabriel is a heavenly messenger well known to Bible students. God sent Gabriel to Daniel,[26] to Zacharias,[27] and to Mary,[28] each with specific messages of supernal significance. In latter-day revelation, Gabriel has been identified as Noah.[29]

The angel Gabriel was the messenger to bring news to Elisabeth and Zacharias that they would be the parents of a baby, later to be known as John the Baptist. Scripture tells us that John "was baptized while he was yet in his childhood, and was ordained by the angel of God . . . to make straight the way of the Lord."[30]

The Bible informs us that John the Baptist was beheaded.[31] His latter-day responsibility to restore the Aaronic Priesthood is also a stunning testimony of the glorious reality of the Resurrection.

The Book of Mormon adds much to our understanding of angels. An instructive example is in chapter seven of Third Nephi: "It came to pass that Nephi—having been visited by angels and also the voice of the Lord, therefore having seen angels, and being eye-witness, . . . that he might know concerning the ministry of Christ, . . . began to testify, boldly, repentance and remission of sins through faith on the Lord Jesus Christ.

" . . . for so great was his faith on the Lord Jesus Christ that angels did minister unto him daily."[32]

Mormon anticipated a question from us, as readers of his ancient record. His question: "Have angels ceased to appear unto the children of men?"

His answer: "Behold I say unto you, Nay; for it is by faith that miracles are wrought; and it is by faith that angels appear and minister unto men."[33]

That specific angels participated in the Restoration is evident from section 128 of the Doctrine and Covenants. There we read about "the voice of God . . . and the voice of Michael, the archangel; the voice of Gabriel, and of Raphael, and of divers angels, from Michael or Adam down to the present time."[34]

Those diverse angels—or heavenly messengers—could include John the Beloved, who did not die, but was allowed to tarry on earth as a ministering servant until the time of the Lord's Second Coming.[35] The three Nephites could likewise be in that same category. Their desire to tarry until the Second Coming was also granted.[36] "They are as the angels of God, and . . . can show themselves unto whatsoever man it seemeth them good."[37]

The Lord made a promise to those faithfully engaged in His service. He said: "I will go before your face. I will be on your right hand and on your left, and my Spirit shall be in your hearts, and mine angels round about you, to bear you up."[38]

My wife Wendy and I are the beneficiaries of that promise. On one occasion, we were attacked by armed men with malicious intent. They announced their purpose: to kidnap her, and to kill me. After they maliciously molested us in those evil objectives, they became totally foiled. A gun to my head failed to fire. And my wife was suddenly released from their hideous grasp. Then they disappeared as quickly as they had appeared. We were mercifully rescued from potential disaster.[39] We know we were protected by angels round about us. Yes, the Lord's precious promise had been invoked in our behalf.

Other angels are also at work. Often our members are "angels" to neighbors in need. Home teachers and visiting teachers, as ordinary people, frequently render service that seems angelic to grateful recipients. Young people who quietly leave homemade goodies on a doorstep or two experience the joy of anonymous service to others. And I am among the many who have often referred to the loving acts of an "angel mother" or an "angel wife," or the priceless love of "angel children."

Do we believe in angels? *Yes!* We believe in angels—heavenly messengers—seen and unseen; and earthly angels who know *whom* to help and *how* to help. Gospel messengers, or angels, can include ordinary people like you and me.

May angels, known and unknown, serve you and protect you along life's perilous journey.

can come to all who choose to

walk in the ways of the Master.

His invitation is expressed in

three loving words:

"Come, follow me."

CHAPTER 2

HE BLESSES US WITH PEACE AND LOVE

When we face difficulties in our lives, it may sometimes seem impossible that we would ever find peace. But peace is made possible by that transcendent gift from our Heavenly Father: "For God so loved the world, that he gave his only begotten Son, that whosoever believeth in him should not perish, but have everlasting life."[1]

Focusing on the Lord and everlasting life can help us through all the challenges of mortality. Imperfect people share Planet Earth with other imperfect people. Ours is a fallen world marred by excessive debt, wars, natural disasters, disease, and death.

Personal challenges come as well. A father may have lost his job. A young mother may have learned of a grave illness. A son or a daughter may have gone astray. Whatever may cause the worry, each of us yearns to find inner peace.

There is only one source of true and lasting peace: Jesus the Christ—our Prince of Peace.[2] This title He bore in addition to others for which He was foreordained.

He was anointed by His Father to be the Savior of the world. These two titles—the Messiah and the Christ—designated His responsibility as the *anointed* one.[3]

Under the direction of His Father, Jesus was Creator of this and other worlds.[4] Jesus is our Advocate with the Father.[5] Jesus was the promised Immanuel,[6] the great I Am and Jehovah of Old Testament times.[7]

He was sent by His Father to accomplish the Atonement, *the* central act of all human history. Because of His Atonement, immortality became a reality for all, and eternal life became a possibility for those who choose to follow Him.[8] These objectives are the work and glory of Almighty God.[9]

As our great Exemplar, Jesus taught us how to live, to love, and to learn. He taught us how to pray, to forgive, and to endure to the end.[10] He taught us how to care about others more than we care about ourselves. He taught us about mercy and kindness—making real changes in our lives through His power. He taught us how to find peace of heart and mind. One day, we will stand before Him as our just Judge and merciful Master.[11]

These sacred responsibilities of the Lord cause us to

adore Him as our personal and perennial Prince of Peace. We praise Him for our privilege as parents, grandparents, and teachers of children. He taught, "Suffer little children, and forbid them not, to come unto me: for of such is the kingdom of heaven."[12]

He can bring peace to those whose lives have been ravaged by war. Families disrupted by military duty bear memories of war, which in my own mind were imbedded during the Korean War. Wars of our present era are more sophisticated, but are still as wrenching to families. Those who so suffer can turn to the Lord. His is the consoling message of peace on earth and good will among men.[13]

Peace can come to those who are not feeling well. Some have bodies that are wounded. Others ache spiritually because of missing loved ones or other emotional trauma. Peace can come to your soul as you build faith in the Prince of Peace.

"Have ye any that are sick among you? Bring them hither. Have ye any that are lame, or blind, or halt, or maimed, . . . or that are afflicted in any manner? Bring them hither and I will heal them."[14]

"I see that your faith is sufficient that I should heal you."[15]

Peace can come to one who suffers in sorrow. Whether sorrow stems from mistakes or from sins, all the Lord requires is real repentance. Scripture pleads with us to "flee [from] youthful lusts; . . . [and] call on the Lord out of a pure heart."[16] Then His soothing "balm in Gilead" can heal us.[17]

Think of the change in John Newton, born in London in 1725. He repented from his sinful life as a slave trader to become an Anglican clergyman. With that mighty change of heart, John wrote words to the hymn "Amazing Grace":

Amazing grace! How sweet the sound
That saved a wretch like me.
I once was lost, but now am found,
Was blind, but now I see.[18]

"Joy shall be in heaven over one sinner that repenteth."[19]

Peace can come to those whose labors are heavy: "Come unto me, all ye that labour and are heavy laden, and I will give you rest.

"Take my yoke upon you, and learn of me; for I am meek and lowly in heart: and ye shall find rest unto your souls.

"For my yoke is easy, and my burden is light."[20]

Peace can come to those who mourn. The Lord said, "Blessed are they that mourn: for they shall be comforted."[21] As we endure the passing of a loved one, we can be filled with the peace of the Lord through the whisperings of the Spirit.

"Those that die in me shall not taste of death, for it shall be sweet unto them."[22]

"Peace I leave with you, my peace I give unto you: not as the world giveth, give I unto you. Let not your heart be troubled, neither let it be afraid."[23]

"I am the resurrection, and the life: he that believeth in me, though he were dead, yet shall he live:

"And whosoever liveth and believeth in me shall never die."[24]

Peace can come to all who earnestly seek the Prince of Peace. His is the sweet and saving message our missionaries take throughout the world. They preach the gospel of Jesus Christ as restored by Him through the Prophet Joseph Smith. Missionaries teach these life-changing words of the Lord: "If ye love me, keep my commandments."[25]

Peace can come to all who choose to walk in the ways of the Master. His invitation is expressed in three loving words: "Come, follow me."[26]

One way we find peace in following Christ is in living the attributes He exemplified. Most Christians are familiar with the attributes of Jesus Christ as reported in the Bible. They marvel at the love He demonstrated for the poor, the sick, and the downtrodden. Those who consider themselves His disciples also strive to emulate His example and follow His beloved Apostle's exhortation: "Let us love one another: for love is of God; and every one that loveth is born of God, and knoweth God. . . . For God is love."[27]

This concept is clarified by the Book of Mormon. It describes *how* one is born of God and *how* one gains the power to love as He does. It identifies three core principles that bring the power of God's love into our lives.

First, the Book of Mormon teaches that exercising faith in Christ and entering into a *covenant* with Him to keep His commandments is the key to being reborn spiritually. To Book of Mormon people who had made such a covenant, King Benjamin remarked, "And now, because of the covenant which ye have made ye shall be called the children of Christ, his sons, and his daughters; for behold, this day he hath spiritually begotten you; for ye say that your hearts are changed through faith on his name; therefore, ye are born of him and have become his sons and his daughters."[28]

Second, the Savior Himself teaches that the power to become more like Him comes through receiving the *ordinances* of the gospel: "Now this is the commandment: Repent, all ye ends of the earth, and come unto me and be baptized in my name, that ye may be sanctified by the reception of the Holy Ghost, that ye may stand spotless before me at the last day."[29]

Third, He exhorts us to *follow His example*: "What manner of men ought ye to be?" He asks. His answer: "Verily I say unto you, even as I am."[30] Truly, He wants us to become more like Him.

Some of the most sublime examples of His love are recorded in the Book of Mormon. These examples can apply in our own lives as we strive to become more like the Lord.

It was His love for Lehi and Lehi's family—and their love for Him—that brought them to the Americas, their promised land, where they prospered.[31]

It was God's love for us that prompted Him centuries ago to command Nephite prophets to keep a sacred record of their people. Lessons from that record relate to our salvation and exaltation. These teachings are now available in the Book of Mormon. This sacred text stands as tangible evidence of God's love for all of His children throughout the world.[32]

It was Christ's love for His "other sheep" that brought Him to the New World.[33] From the Book of Mormon we learn that great natural disasters and three days of darkness occurred in the New World following the death of the Lord in the Old World. Then the glorified and resurrected Lord descended from heaven and ministered among the people of the New World.

"I am the light and the life of the world," He told them, "and I have drunk out of that bitter cup which the Father hath given me, and have glorified the Father in taking upon me the sins of the world."[34]

Then He provided one of the most intimate experiences anyone could have with Him. He invited them to feel the wound in His side and the prints of the nails in His hands and feet, that they would know for certain that He was "the God of Israel, and the God of the whole earth, and [had] been slain for the sins of the world."[35]

Jesus then gave His disciples the authority to baptize, to bestow the gift of the Holy Ghost, and to administer the sacrament. He gave them the power to establish His Church among them, led by twelve disciples.

He delivered to them some of the foundational teachings He had given His disciples in the Old World. He healed their sick. He knelt and prayed to the Father in words so powerful and sacred they could not be recorded. So powerful was His prayer that those who heard Him were overcome with joy. Overcome by His love for them and by their faith in Him, Jesus Himself wept. He prophesied of God's work in the centuries leading up to the promised advent of His Second Coming.[36]

Then He asked them to bring their children to Him.

"And he took their little children, one by one, and blessed them, and prayed unto the Father for them.

"And when he had done this he wept again;

"And he spake unto the multitude, and said unto them: Behold your little ones.

"And as they looked to behold they cast their eyes towards heaven, and they saw the heavens open, and they saw angels descending out of heaven as it were in the midst of fire; and they came down and encircled those little ones about, . . . and the angels did minister unto them."[37] Such is the purity and power of God's love, as revealed in the Book of Mormon.

In these latter days we who are privileged to have the Book of Mormon, to be members of the Lord's Church, to have His gospel, and to keep His commandments know something of God's infinite love. We know how to make His love our own. As we become His true disciples, we gain the power to love as He does. As we keep His commandments, we become more like Him. We broaden our personal circle of love in reaching out to people of every nation, kindred, and tongue.

We'll sing all hail to the Prince of Peace and Love![38] For He will come again. Then "the glory of the Lord shall be revealed, and all flesh shall see it together."[39] As the Millennial Messiah, He will reign as King of kings, and Lord of lords.[40]

As we follow Jesus Christ, He will lead us to live with Him and our Heavenly Father, with our families. Through our many challenges of mortality, if we remain faithful to covenants made, if we endure to the end, we will qualify for that greatest of all the gifts of God, eternal life.[41]

In this life and in the next,
SPIRIT AND BODY,
when joined together,
become a living soul of supernal worth.

CHAPTER 3

HE GIVES US PHYSICAL AND SPIRITUAL GIFTS

Recently, Sister Nelson and I enjoyed the beauty of tropical fish in a small private aquarium. Fish with vivid colors and of a variety of shapes and sizes darted back and forth. I asked the attendant nearby, "Who provides food for these beautiful fish?"

She responded, "I do."

Then I asked, "Have they ever thanked you?"

She replied, "Not yet!"

I thought of some people I know who are just as oblivious to their Creator and their true "bread of life."[1] They live from day to day without an awareness of God and His goodness unto them. They fail to recognize His help in accomplishing what would otherwise be impossible.

How much better it would be if all could be more aware of God's providence and love, and would express that gratitude to Him. Ammon taught, "Let us give thanks to [God], for he doth work righteousness forever."[2] Our degree of gratitude is a measure of our love for Him.

God is the Father of our spirits.[3] He has a glorified, perfected body of flesh and bone.[4] We lived with Him in heaven before we were born.[5] And when He created us physically, we were created in the image of God, each with a personal body.[6]

Think of our physical sustenance. It is truly heaven-sent. The necessities of air, food, and water all come to us as gifts from a loving Heavenly Father. The earth was created to support our brief sojourn in mortality.[7] We were born with a capacity to grow, love, marry, and form families.

Marriage and family are ordained of God. The family is the most important social unit in time and in eternity. Under God's great plan of happiness, families can be sealed in temples and be prepared to return to dwell in His holy presence forever. This fulfills the deepest longings of the human soul—the natural yearning for endless association with beloved members of one's family.

We are part of His divine purpose: "My work and my glory," He said, is "to bring to pass the immortality and eternal life of man."[8] In order to achieve those objectives, "God . . . gave his only begotten Son, that whosoever believeth in him should not perish, but have everlasting life."[9] That act was a supernal manifestation of God´s love. "For [He] sent not his Son into the world to condemn the world; but that the world through him might be saved."[10]

Central to God's eternal plan is the mission of His Son Jesus Christ.[11] He came to redeem God's children.[12] Because of the Lord's Atonement, resurrection (or immortality) became a reality.[13] Because of the Atonement, eternal life became a possibility for all who would qualify. Jesus so explained: "I am the resurrection, and the life: he that believeth in me, though he were dead, yet shall he live:

"And whosoever liveth and believeth in me shall never die."[14]

For the Atonement of the Lord and His gift of resurrection—thanks be to God!

Our Heavenly Father loves His children.[15] He has blessed each with physical and spiritual gifts. Let me speak of each type. When you sing "I Am a Child of God," think of His gift to you of your own physical body. The many amazing attributes of your body attest to your own "divine nature."[16]

Each organ of your body is a wondrous gift from God. Each eye has an auto-focusing lens. Nerves and muscles control two eyes to make a single three-dimensional image. The eyes are connected to the brain, which records the sights seen.

Your heart is an incredible pump.[17] It has four delicate

valves that control the direction of blood flow. These valves open and close more than 100,000 times a day—36 million times a year. Yet, unless altered by disease, they are able to withstand such stress almost indefinitely.

Think of the body's defense system. To protect it from harm, it perceives pain. In response to infection, it generates antibodies. The skin provides protection. It warns against injury that excessive heat or cold might cause.

The body renews its own outdated cells and regulates the levels of its own vital ingredients. The body heals its cuts, bruises, and broken bones. Its capacity for reproduction is another sacred gift from God.

We should remember that a perfect body is not required to achieve one's divine destiny. In fact, some of the sweetest spirits are housed in frail or imperfect bodies. Great spiritual strength is often developed by people with physical challenges, precisely because they are so challenged.

Anyone who studies the workings of the human body has surely "seen God moving in his majesty and power."[18] Because the body is governed by divine law, any healing comes by obedience to the law upon which that blessing is predicated.[19]

Yet some people erroneously think that these marvelous physical attributes happened by chance or resulted from an accident somewhere. Ask yourself, "Could an explosion in a printing shop produce a dictionary?" The likelihood is *most* remote. But if so, it could never heal its own torn pages or reproduce its own newer editions!

If the body's capacity for normal function, defense, repair, regulation, and regeneration were to prevail without limit, life here would continue in perpetuity. Yes, we would be stranded here on earth! Mercifully for us, our Creator provided for aging and other processes that would ultimately result in our physical death. Death, like birth, is part of life. Scripture teaches that "it was not expedient that man should be reclaimed from this temporal death, for that would destroy the great plan of happiness."[20] To return to God through the gateway we call death is a joy for those who love Him and are prepared to meet Him.[21] Eventually the time will come when each "spirit and . . . body shall be reunited again in . . . perfect form; both limb and joint shall be restored to its proper frame,"[22] never to be separated again. For these physical gifts, thanks be to God!

Important as is the body, it serves as a tabernacle for one's eternal spirit. Our spirits existed in the premortal realm[23] and will continue to live after the body dies.[24] The spirit provides the body with animation and personality.[25] In this life and in the next, spirit and body, when joined together, become a living soul of supernal worth.

Because one's spirit is so important, its development is of

eternal consequence. It is strengthened as we communicate in humble prayer with our loving Heavenly Father.[26]

The attributes by which we shall be judged one day are all spiritual.[27] These include love, virtue, integrity, compassion, and service to others.[28] Your spirit, coupled with and housed in your body, is able to develop and manifest these attributes in ways that are vital to your eternal progression.[29] Spiritual progress is attained through the steps of faith, repentance, baptism, the gift of the Holy Ghost, and enduring to the end, including the endowment and sealing ordinances of the holy temple.[30]

Just as the body requires daily food for survival, the spirit needs nourishment as well. The spirit is nurtured by eternal truth. It has not been long since we celebrated the 400th anniversary of the King James translation of the Holy Bible. And we have had the Book of Mormon for nearly 200 years. It has now been translated in its entirety or as selections into 107 languages. Because of these and other precious scriptures, we know that God is our Eternal Father and that His Son Jesus Christ is our Savior and Redeemer. For these spiritual gifts, thanks be to God!

We know that prophets of many dispensations, such as Adam, Noah, Moses, and Abraham, all taught of the divinity of our Heavenly Father and of Jesus Christ. Our present dispensation was introduced by Heavenly Father and Jesus

Christ, when They appeared to the Prophet Joseph Smith in 1820. The Church was organized in 1830. We remain under covenant today to take the gospel to "every nation, kindred, tongue, and people."[31] As we do so, both givers and receivers will be blessed.

Ours is the responsibility to teach His children and awaken in them an awareness of God. Long ago, King Benjamin said, "Believe in God; believe that he is, and that he created all things, both in heaven and in earth; believe that he has all wisdom, and all power, both in heaven and in earth; . . .

" . . . Believe that ye must repent of your sins and forsake them, and humble yourselves before God; and ask in sincerity of heart that he would forgive you; and now, if you believe all these things see that ye do them."[32]

God is the same yesterday, today, and forever, but we are not. Each day, ours is the challenge to access the power of the Atonement, so that we can truly change, become more Christlike, and qualify for the gift of exaltation and live eternally with God, Jesus Christ, and our families.[33] For these powers, privileges, and gospel gifts, thanks be to God!

for mutual understanding

and

respect between ourselves

and our neighbors.

If we really care for others,

WE SHOULD PRAY FOR THEM.

CHAPTER 4

HE TEACHES US TO PRAY

One way we enlist the Lord's help in accomplishing the impossible is by praying for it. As in all things, our Savior set the example for us in this important principle of prayer.

Our prayers follow patterns and teachings of the Lord Jesus Christ. He taught us how to pray. From His prayers we can learn many important lessons. We can begin with the Lord's Prayer and add lessons from other prayers He has given.[1]

As we review the Lord's Prayer, listen for lessons:

"Our Father which art in heaven, Hallowed be thy name.

"Thy kingdom come. Thy will be done in earth, as it is in heaven.

"Give us this day our daily bread.

"And forgive us our debts, as we forgive our debtors.

"And lead us not into temptation, but deliver us from evil: For thine is the kingdom, and the power, and the glory, for ever. Amen."[2]

The Lord's Prayer is recorded twice in the New Testament and once in the Book of Mormon.[3] It is also included in the Joseph Smith Translation of the Bible,[4] where clarification is provided by these two phrases:

1. "Forgive us our trespasses, as we forgive those who trespass against us,"[5] and

2. "Suffer us not to be led into temptation, but deliver us from evil."[6]

The clarification on forgiveness is supported by other statements of the Master. He said to His servants, "Inasmuch as you have forgiven one another your trespasses, even so I, the Lord, forgive you."[7] In other words, if one is to be forgiven, one must first forgive.[8] The clarification on temptation is helpful, for surely we would *not* be led into temptation by Deity. The Lord said, "Watch and pray, that ye enter not into temptation."[9]

Though the four versions of the Lord's Prayer are not identical, they all open with a salutation to "Our Father," signifying a close relationship between God and His children. The phrase "hallowed be thy name" reflects the respect and worshipful attitude that we should feel as we pray. "Thy will be done" expresses a concept that we will discuss later.

His request for "daily bread" includes a need for spiritual nourishment as well. Jesus, who called Himself "the bread of life," gave a promise: "He that cometh to me shall never hunger."[10] And as we partake of sacramental emblems worthily, we are further promised that we may always have His Spirit to be with us.[11] That is spiritual sustenance that cannot be obtained in any other way.

As the Lord closes His prayer, He acknowledges God's great power and glory, ending with "Amen." Our prayers also close with *amen*. Though it is pronounced differently in various languages, its meaning is the same. It means "truly" or "verily."[12] Adding *amen* solemnly affirms a sermon or a prayer.[13] Those who concur should each add an audible amen[14] to signify "that is my solemn declaration too."[15]

The Lord prefaced His prayer by first asking His followers to avoid "vain repetitions"[16] and to pray "after this manner."[17] Thus, the Lord's Prayer serves as a pattern to follow and not as a piece to memorize and recite repetitively. The Master simply wants us to pray for God's help while we strive constantly to resist evil and live righteously.

Other prayers of the Lord are also instructive, especially His intercessory prayers. They are so named because the Lord prayerfully interceded with His Father for the benefit of His disciples. Picture in your mind the Savior of the world kneeling in prayer, as I quote from John chapter 17:

"These words spake Jesus, and lifted up his eyes to heaven, and said, Father, . . . glorify thy Son, that thy Son also may glorify thee. . . .

" . . . I have finished the work which thou gavest me to do. . . .

"For I have given unto them the words which thou gavest me; and they have received them, and have known surely that I came out from thee, and they have believed that thou didst send me.

"I pray for them."[18]

From this prayer of the Lord we learn how keenly He feels His responsibility as our Mediator and Advocate with the Father.[19] Just as keenly, we should feel our responsibility to keep His commandments and endure to the end.[20]

An intercessory prayer was also given by Jesus for the people of ancient America. The record states that "no one can conceive of the joy which filled our souls at the time we heard him pray for us unto the Father."[21] Then Jesus added: "Blessed are ye because of your faith. And now behold, my joy is full."[22]

In a later prayer, Jesus included a plea for unity. "Father," He said, "I pray unto thee for them, . . . that they may believe in me, that I may be in them as thou, Father, art in me, that we may be one."[23] We too can pray for unity. We can pray to be of one heart and one mind with the Lord's anointed and with our loved ones. We can pray for mutual understanding and respect between ourselves and our neighbors. If we really care for others, we should pray for them.[24] "Pray one for another, " taught James, for "the effectual fervent prayer of a righteous man availeth much."[25]

Other lessons about prayer were taught by the Lord. He told His disciples that "ye must always pray unto the Father in my name."[26] The Savior further emphasized, "Pray in your families unto the Father, always in my name."[27] Obediently, we apply that lesson when we pray to our Heavenly Father in the name of Jesus Christ.[28]

Another of the Lord's prayers teaches a lesson repeated in three consecutive verses:

"Father, I thank thee that thou hast given the Holy Ghost unto these whom I have chosen. . . .

"Father, I pray thee that thou wilt give the Holy Ghost unto all them that shall believe in their words.

"Father, thou hast given them the Holy Ghost because they believe in me."[29]

If companionship of the Holy Ghost is that important, we should pray for it too. We should likewise help all converts and our children cultivate the gift of the Holy Ghost. As we so pray, the Holy Ghost can become a vital force for good in our lives.[30]

The Lord has taught ways by which our prayers can be

enhanced. For example, He said that "the song of the righteous is a prayer unto me, and it shall be answered with a blessing upon their heads."[31]

Prayer can also be enhanced by fasting.[32] The Lord said, "I give unto you a commandment that ye shall continue in prayer and fasting from this time forth."[33] A plea for wisdom in fasting was offered by President Joseph F. Smith, who cautioned that "there is such a thing as overdoing. A man may fast and pray till he kills himself; and there isn't any necessity for it; nor wisdom in it. . . . The Lord can hear a simple prayer, offered in faith, in half a dozen words, and he will recognize fasting that may not continue more than twenty-four hours, just as readily and as effectually as He will answer a prayer of a thousand words and fasting for a month. . . . The Lord will accept that which is enough, with a good deal more pleasure and satisfaction than that which is too much and unnecessary."[34]

The concept of "too much and unnecessary" could also apply to the length of our prayers. A closing prayer in a Church meeting need not include a summary of each message and should not become an unscheduled sermon. Private prayers can be as long as we want, but public prayers ought to be short supplications for the Spirit of the Lord to be with us or brief declarations of gratitude for what has transpired.

Our prayers can be enhanced in other ways. We can use

"right words"[35]—special pronouns—in reference to Deity. While worldly manners of daily dress and speech are becoming more casual, we have been asked to protect the formal, proper language of prayer. In our prayers we use the respectful pronouns *Thee, Thou, Thy,* and *Thine* instead of *You, Your,* and *Yours.*[36] Doing so helps us to be humble. That can also enhance our prayers. Scripture so declares, "Be thou humble; and the Lord thy God shall lead thee by the hand, and give thee answer to thy prayers."[37]

Prayer begins with individual initiative. "Behold," saith the Lord, "I stand at the door, and knock: if any man hear my voice, and open the door, I will come in to him, and will sup with him, and he with me."[38] That door is opened when we pray to our Heavenly Father in the name of Jesus Christ.[39]

When should we pray? Whenever we desire! Alma taught, "Counsel with the Lord in all thy doings, and he will direct thee for good; yea, when thou liest down at night lie down unto the Lord, . . . and when thou risest in the morning let thy heart be full of thanks unto God; and if ye do these things, ye shall be lifted up at the last day."[40]

Jesus reminded His disciples "that they should not cease to pray in their hearts."[41]

The practice of Church members is to kneel in family prayer each morning and evening, in addition to having daily personal prayers and blessings on our food.[42] President

Thomas S. Monson has said, "As we offer unto the Lord our family and our personal prayers, let us do so with faith and trust in Him."[43] And so, in praying for temporal and spiritual blessings, we should all plead, as did Jesus in the Lord's Prayer, "Thy will be done."[44]

Jesus Christ, the Savior of the world—He who ransomed us with His blood—is our Redeemer and our Exemplar.[45] At the close of His mortal mission, He prayed that His will—as the Beloved Son—might be "swallowed up in the will of the Father."[46] In that crucial hour the Savior cried, "Father, . . . not as I will, but as thou wilt."[47] So we should pray to God, "Thy will be done."

And let us ever pray "that [the Lord's] kingdom may go forth upon the earth, that the inhabitants . . . may . . . be prepared for the days . . . [when] the Son of Man shall come down . . . in the brightness of his glory, to meet the kingdom of God which is set up on the earth."[48]

In our daily lives and in our own crucial hours, may we fervently apply these precious lessons from the Lord, I pray.

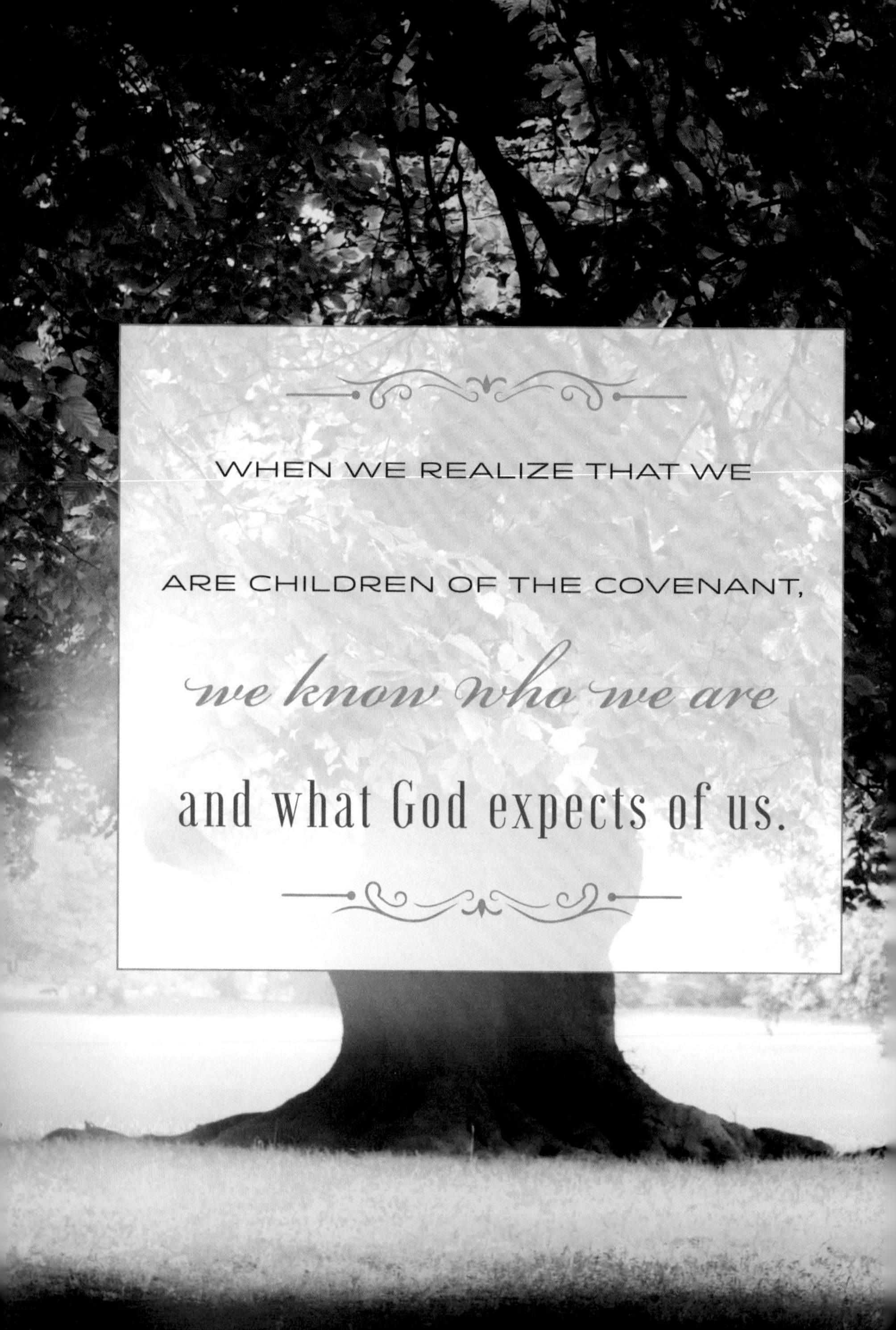
WHEN WE REALIZE THAT WE
ARE CHILDREN OF THE COVENANT,
we know who we are
and what God expects of us.

CHAPTER 5

HE OFFERS COVENANTS TO STRENGTHEN US

One week after I fulfilled an assignment to create the first stake in Moscow, Russia,[1] I attended a district conference in St. Petersburg. While speaking about my gratitude for early missionaries and local leaders who brought strength to the Church in Russia, I mentioned the name of Vyacheslav Efimov. He was the first Russian convert to become a mission president. He and his wife did wonderfully well in that assignment. Not long after they had completed their mission, and much to our sorrow, President Efimov suddenly passed away.[2] He was only fifty-two years of age.

While speaking of this pioneering couple, I felt impressed to ask the congregation if Sister Efimov might be present. Far in the rear of the room a woman stood. I invited her to come to the microphone. Yes, it was Sister Galina Efimov. She spoke with conviction and bore a powerful testimony of the

Lord, of His gospel, and of His restored Church. She and her husband had been sealed in the holy temple. She said they were united forever. They were still missionary companions, she on this side of the veil, and he on the other side.[3] With tears of joy, she thanked God for sacred temple covenants. I wept too, with full realization that the everlasting unity exemplified by this faithful couple was the righteous result of making, keeping, and honoring sacred covenants.

One of the most important concepts of revealed religion is that of a sacred covenant. In legal language, a covenant generally denotes an agreement between two or more parties. But in a religious context, a covenant is much more significant. It is a sacred promise with God. He fixes the terms. Each person may choose to accept those terms. If one accepts the terms of the covenant and obeys God's law, he or she receives the blessings associated with the covenant. We know that "when we obtain any blessing from God, it is by obedience to that law upon which it is predicated."[4]

Through the ages, God has made covenants with His children.[5] His covenants occur throughout the entire plan of salvation and are therefore part of the fulness of His gospel.[6] For example, God promised to send a Savior for His children,[7] asking in turn for their obedience to His law.[8]

In the Bible we read of men and women in the Old World who were identified as children of the covenant. What covenant? "The covenant which God made with [their] fathers, saying unto Abraham, And in thy seed shall all the kindreds of the earth be blessed."[9]

In the Book of Mormon we read of people in the New World who were also identified as children of the covenant.[10] The resurrected Lord so informed them: "Behold, ye are the children of the prophets; and ye are of the house of Israel; and ye are of the covenant which the Father made with your fathers, saying unto Abraham: And in thy seed shall all the kindreds of the earth be blessed."[11]

The Savior explained the importance of their identity as children of the covenant. He said, "The Father having raised me up unto you first, . . . sent me to bless you in turning away every one of you from his iniquities; and this because ye are the children of the covenant."[12]

The covenant God made with Abraham and later reaffirmed with Isaac and Jacob is of transcendent significance. It contained several promises, including:

- Jesus the Christ would be born through Abraham's lineage.
- Abraham's posterity would be numerous, entitled to an eternal increase and also entitled to bear the priesthood.
- Abraham would become a father of many nations.
- Certain lands would be inherited by his posterity.

- All nations of the earth would be blessed by his seed.
- And that covenant would be everlasting—even through "a thousand generations."[13]

Some of these promises have been fulfilled; others are still pending. I quote from an early Book of Mormon prophecy: "Our father [Lehi] hath not spoken of our seed alone, but also of all the house of Israel, pointing to the covenant which should be fulfilled *in the latter days;* which covenant the Lord made to our father Abraham."[14] Isn't that amazing? Some 600 years *before* Jesus was born in Bethlehem, prophets knew that the Abrahamic covenant would be finally fulfilled only *in the latter days.*

To facilitate that promise, the Lord appeared in these latter days to renew that Abrahamic covenant. To the Prophet Joseph Smith the Master declared: "Abraham received promises concerning his seed, and of the fruit of his loins—from whose loins ye are, . . . my servant Joseph. . . . This promise is yours also, because ye are of Abraham."[15]

With this renewal, we have received, as did they of old, the holy priesthood and the everlasting gospel. We have the right to receive the fulness of the gospel, enjoy the blessings of the priesthood, and qualify for God's greatest blessing—that of eternal life.[16]

Some of us are the literal seed of Abraham; others are

gathered into his family by adoption. The Lord makes no distinction.[17] Together we receive these promised blessings—if we seek the Lord and obey His commandments.[18] But if we don't, we lose the blessings of the covenant.[19] To assist us, His Church provides patriarchal blessings to give each recipient a vision for his or her future, as well as a connection with the past, even a declaration of lineage back to Abraham, Isaac, and Jacob.[20]

Brethren of the covenant have the right to qualify for the oath and covenant of the priesthood.[21] If you are "faithful unto the obtaining these two priesthoods, . . . and the magnifying [of your] calling, [you] are sanctified by the Spirit unto the renewing of [your] bodies."[22] That is not all. Men who worthily receive the priesthood receive the Lord Jesus Christ and those who receive the Lord receive God the Father.[23] And those who receive the Father receive all that He has.[24] Incredible blessings flow from this oath and covenant to worthy men, women, and children in all the world.

Ours is the responsibility to help fulfill the Abrahamic covenant. Ours is the seed foreordained and prepared to bless all people of the world.[25] That is why priesthood duty includes missionary work. After some four thousand years of anticipation and preparation, this is the appointed day when the gospel is to be taken to the kindreds of the earth. This is the time of the promised gathering of Israel. And we get to participate! Isn't that exciting? The Lord is counting on those who worthily serve as missionaries in this great time of the gathering of Israel.

The Book of Mormon is a tangible sign that the Lord has commenced to gather His children of covenant Israel.[26] This book, written for *our* day, states as one of its purposes that "ye may know that the covenant which the Father hath made with the children of Israel . . . is already beginning to be fulfilled. . . . For behold, the Lord will remember his covenant which he hath made unto his people of the house of Israel."[27]

Indeed, the Lord has not forgotten! He has blessed us and others throughout the world with the Book of Mormon. One of its purposes is for "the convincing of the Jew and Gentile that Jesus is the Christ."[28] It helps us to make covenants with God. It invites us to remember Him and to know His Beloved Son. It is another testament of Jesus Christ.

Children of the covenant have the right to receive His doctrine and to know the plan of salvation. They *claim* it by making covenants of sacred significance. Brigham Young said: "All Latter-day Saints enter the new and everlasting covenant when they enter this Church. . . . They enter the new and everlasting covenant to sustain the Kingdom of God."[29] They *keep* the covenant by obedience to His commandments.

Commitment keeping prepares a person for covenant keeping. The gospel of Jesus Christ includes the making and keeping of sacred covenants, the first of which is the covenant of baptism. The act of baptism itself does not wash sin away. Thanks to the Atonement, one becomes clean when one faithfully keeps the baptismal covenant to follow the Lord Jesus Christ.

Next comes the gift of the Holy Ghost. What a blessing that is! Like all gifts, it needs to be unwrapped and used.

Then we come to the culminating covenants of our mortality: the endowment and sealing ordinances of the temple.

"Whenever the Lord has had a people on the earth who will obey His word, they have been commanded to build temples."[30] Temple patterns are as old as human life on earth. Actually, the plan for temples was established even *before* the foundation of the world, when provision was made for the redemption of those who might die without a knowledge of the gospel.[31]

Adam and Eve were instructed by the Lord to build an altar and offer sacrifices.[32] The tabernacle of Moses was a portable precursor.[33] Then came that temple built in the days of Solomon. It was destroyed in 600 B.C. and restored by Zerubbabel about a hundred years later. It was burned in 37 B.C. and rebuilt by King Herod.

This was the temple that Jesus knew and loved. But He did not love the way the people defiled the temple. At the first cleansing, Jesus reverently referred to the temple as "my Father's house."[34] At the time of the second cleansing of the temple, He called it "my house."[35] Later, when He foresaw the temple being further desecrated, Jesus called it "your house . . . left unto you desolate."[36] That prophecy was fulfilled when the temple was destroyed by the Romans in A.D. 70.

Several years ago, I was in Jerusalem being guided through excavations tunneled to the left of the present so-called "Wailing Wall." There, in that tunnel, Jewish rabbis were praying for the day when the third temple would be built in Jerusalem. I was told that one of them had asked Israel's famous archeologist, Yigael Yadin, what they would do with a new temple if it were built in Jerusalem. He reportedly replied, "I don't know. Ask the Mormons. They'll know!"

Indeed we do know! Temples are an essential component of the Restoration of the gospel in its fulness.

After decades of spiritual darkness came the beginning of the Restoration. In 1820, God the Father and His Son, Jesus Christ, appeared to the Prophet Joseph Smith. Later, They directed him to build the first temple of this new and final dispensation of the fulness of times. It was built in Kirtland, Ohio. It was a preparatory temple, where important keys of the priesthood were conferred upon human beings. The next temple, the Nauvoo Temple, had a baptismal font provided so that Saints could be baptized vicariously for their deceased ancestors.[37]

President Brigham Young, shortly after he arrived in the valley of the Great Salt Lake, touched his cane to the desert soil and proclaimed, "Here we will build a temple to our God."[38]

Year by year and step by step, revelation has come to successive prophets. President Wilford Woodruff taught this concept when speaking in general conference in April 1894: "[Joseph Smith and Brigham Young] did not receive all the revelations that belong to [temple] work; neither did President Taylor, nor has Wilford Woodruff. There will be no end to this work until it is perfected."[39]

At the dedication of the St. George Temple on January 1, 1877, the very year that President Young passed away, he said: "What do you suppose the fathers would say if they could speak from the dead? Would they not say, 'We have lain here thousands of years, here in this prison house, waiting for this dispensation to come?' . . . What would they whisper in our ears? Why, if they had the power the very thunders of heaven would be in our ears, if we could but realize the importance of the work we are engaged in. All the angels in heaven are looking at this little handful of people, and stimulating them to the salvation of the human family.

. . . When I think upon this subject, I want the tongues of seven thunders to wake up the people."[40]

President Howard W. Hunter added this statement: "I invite the Latter-day Saints to look to the temple of the Lord as the great symbol of [their] membership. It is the deepest desire of my heart to have every member of the Church worthy to enter the temple. It would please the Lord if every adult member would be worthy of—and carry—a current temple recommend."[41]

Why do we have temples? Why do we have missionaries? Why should anyone join this Church? To make life more pleasant, satisfying, or uplifting? Yes, but other organizations can also do some of that. In fact, we join this Church to make and keep sacred covenants that will qualify us for eternal life. We join this Church so that our families can be together forever. Only the Lord's Church can offer these enduring blessings.

Without sealing ordinances performed for families in the temple, the whole earth would be utterly wasted![42] The purposes of the Creation, the Fall, and the Atonement would all be frustrated.

I repeat: God simply wants His children to return to Him. For this to happen, each of us needs to make and keep sacred covenants, receive the ordinances of salvation and exaltation, and be linked to both our ancestors and our posterity. Only then are we qualified to dwell with Deity and our families forever.

When we realize that we are children of the covenant, we know who we are and what God expects of us.[43] His law is written in our hearts.[44] He is our God and we are His people.[45] Committed children of the covenant remain steadfast, even in the midst of adversity. When that doctrine is deeply implanted in our hearts, even the sting of death is soothed and our spiritual stamina is strengthened.

The greatest compliment that can be earned here in this life is to be known as a covenant keeper. The rewards for a covenant keeper will be realized both here and hereafter. Scripture declares that "ye should consider on the blessed and happy state of those that keep the commandments of God. For behold, they are blessed in all things, . . . and if they hold out faithful to the end they are received into heaven, . . . [and] dwell with God in a state of never-ending happiness."[46]

God lives. Jesus is the Christ. His Church has been restored to bless all people. And we, as *faithful* children of the covenant, will be blessed now and forever.

WHAT WE CAN DO

THE GIFT OF SPIRITUAL DISCERNMENT

is a supernal gift.

It allows members of the Church

 to see things not visible 

and to feel things not tangible.

CHAPTER 6

WE CAN RECEIVE REVELATION

I am thankful for the miracle of modern communication that allows Church leaders to reach millions of people throughout the world. Today's technology also allows us to use wireless telephones to exchange information rapidly. Wendy and I were on assignment on another continent when we learned that a new baby had arrived in our extended family. We received the good news minutes after that birth had occurred half a world away.

Even more amazing than modern technology is our opportunity to access information directly from heaven, without hardware, software, or monthly service fees. It is one of the most marvelous gifts the Lord has offered to mortals. It is His generous invitation to "*ask,* and it shall be given you; *seek,* and ye shall find; *knock,* and it shall be opened unto you."[1]

This timeless offer to provide personal revelation is extended to all of His children. It almost sounds too good to be true. But it is true! I have received and responded to that heavenly help. And I have learned that I always need to be ready to receive it.

Years ago, while immersed in the task of preparing a talk for general conference, I was aroused from a sound sleep with an idea impressed strongly upon my mind. Immediately I reached for pencil and paper near my bed and wrote as rapidly as I could. I went back to sleep, knowing I had captured that great impression. The next morning I looked at that piece of paper and found, much to my dismay, that my writing was totally illegible! I still keep pencil and paper at my bedside, but I write more carefully now.

To access information from heaven, one must first have a firm faith and a deep desire. One needs to "ask with a sincere heart, [and] real intent, having faith in Jesus Christ."[2] "Real intent" means that one *really intends* to follow the divine direction given.

The next requirement is to study the matter diligently. This concept was taught to leaders of this restored Church when they were first learning how to gain personal revelation. The Lord instructed them, "I say unto you, that you must study it out in your mind; then you must ask me if it be right, and if it is right I will cause that your bosom shall burn within you; therefore, you shall feel that it is right."[3]

Part of being prepared is to know and obey the relevant teachings of the Lord. Some of His timeless truths are applicable generally, such as the commandments not to steal, not to kill, and not to bear false witness. Other teachings or commandments are also general, such as those regarding the Sabbath, the sacrament, baptism, and confirmation.

Some revelations have been given for unique circumstances, such as Noah's building of the ark or the necessity for prophets like Moses, Lehi, and Brigham Young to lead their followers in arduous travel. God's long-established pattern of teaching His children through prophets assures us that He will bless each prophet and that He will bless those who heed prophetic counsel.

A desire to follow the prophet requires much effort because the natural man knows very little of God and even less of His prophet. Paul wrote that "the natural man [receives] not the things of the Spirit of God: for they are foolishness unto him: neither can he know them, because they are spiritually discerned."[4] The change from being a natural man to a devoted disciple is a mighty one.[5]

Another prophet taught that "the natural man is an enemy to God, and has been from the fall of Adam, and will be, forever and ever, unless he yields to the enticings of the Holy

Spirit, and putteth off the natural man and becometh a saint through the atonement of Christ the Lord, and becometh as a child, submissive, meek, humble, patient, full of love, willing to submit to all things which the Lord seeth fit to inflict upon him, even as a child doth submit to his father."[6]

Recently I observed such a mighty change in a man whom I first met about ten years ago. He had come to a stake conference at which his son was sustained as a member of the new stake presidency. This father was not a member of the Church. After his son had been set apart, I put my arms around this father and praised him for having such a wonderful son. Then I boldly declared: "The day will come when you will want to have this son sealed to you and your wife in a holy temple. And when that day comes, I would be honored to perform that sealing for you."

During the subsequent decade, I did not see this man. Then one day he and his wife came to my office. He greeted me warmly and recounted how startled he was with my earlier invitation. He didn't do much about it until later, when his hearing began to fail. Then he awakened to the realization that his body was changing and that his time on earth was indeed limited. In due course he ultimately lost his hearing. At the same time, he became converted and joined the Church.

During our visit he summarized his total transformation:

"I had to lose my hearing before I could heed the great importance of your message. Then I realized how much I wanted my loved ones to be sealed to me. I am now worthy and prepared. Will you please perform that sealing?" This I did with a deep sense of gratitude to God.

After such a conversion takes place, even further spiritual refinement can come. Personal revelation can be honed to become spiritual discernment. To *discern* means to sift, to separate, or to distinguish.[7] The gift of spiritual discernment is a supernal gift.[8] It allows members of the Church to see things not visible and to feel things not tangible.

Bishops are entitled to that gift as they face the task of seeking out the poor and caring for the needy. With that gift, sisters and brothers may view trends in the world and detect those that, however popular, are shallow or even dangerous. Members can discern between schemes that are flashy and fleeting and those refinements that are uplifting and enduring.

Discernment was implicit in important instructions President John Taylor gave long ago.[9] He taught stake presidents, bishops, and others: "It is the right of those holding [these positions] to obtain the word of God with regard to the duties of their presidencies that they may more effectually carry out His holy purposes. None of the callings or positions in the priesthood are intended for the personal benefits, emoluments and fame of those who hold them, but are expressly given to fulfil the purposes of our Heavenly Father and build up the Kingdom of God upon the earth. . . . We . . . seek to understand the will of God, and then carry it out; and see that it is carried out by those over whom we have the charge."[10]

For you to receive individual revelation unique to your own needs and responsibilities, certain guidelines prevail. The Lord asks you to develop "faith, hope, charity and love, with an eye single to the glory of God." Then with your firm "faith, virtue, knowledge, temperance, patience, brotherly kindness, godliness, charity, humility, [and] diligence," you may *ask,* and you will receive; you may *knock,* and it will be opened unto you.[11]

Revelation from God is always compatible with His eternal law. It never contradicts His doctrine. It is facilitated by proper reverence for Deity. The Master gave this instruction:

"I, the Lord, am merciful and gracious unto those who fear me, and delight to honor those who serve me in righteousness and in truth unto the end.

"Great shall be their reward and eternal shall be their glory.

"To them will I reveal all mysteries [and] my will concerning all things pertaining to my kingdom."[12]

Revelation need not all come at once. It may be

incremental. "Saith the Lord God: I will give unto the children of men line upon line, precept upon precept, here a little and there a little; and blessed are those who hearken unto my precepts, and lend an ear unto my counsel, for they shall learn wisdom; for unto him that receiveth I will give more."[13] Patience and perseverance are part of our eternal progression.

Prophets have described what they felt while receiving revelation. Joseph Smith and Oliver Cowdery reported that "the veil was taken from our minds, and the eyes of our understanding were opened."[14] President Joseph F. Smith wrote, "As I pondered over these things which are written, the eyes of my understanding were opened, and the Spirit of the Lord rested upon me."[15]

Every Latter-day Saint may merit personal revelation. The invitation to ask, seek, and knock for divine direction exists because God lives and Jesus is the living Christ. It exists because this is His living Church.[16] And we are blessed today to be led by living prophets. That we may hearken to and heed their prophetic counsel is my prayer.

A pivotal spiritual attribute is that of

self-mastery—

THE STRENGTH TO PLACE

REASON OVER APPETITE.

CHAPTER 7

WE CAN OVERCOME TEMPTATION

In this world, each day is a day of decision. President Thomas S. Monson has taught us that "decisions determine destiny."[1] The wise use of your freedom to make your own decisions is crucial to your spiritual growth, now and for eternity. You are never too young to learn, never too old to change. Your yearnings to learn and change come from a divinely instilled striving for eternal progression.[2] Each day brings opportunity for decisions that will affect our eternity.

We are eternal beings—spirit children of heavenly parents. The Bible records that "God created man in his own image, . . . male and female created he them."[3] Recently I heard a chorus of children sing the beloved song "I Am a Child of God."[4] I wondered, "Why haven't I heard that song rendered more often by singing mothers or faithful fathers?"

Are we not *all* children of God? In truth, not one of us can *ever stop* being a child of God!

As children of God, we should love Him with all our heart and soul, even more than we love our earthly parents.[5] We should love our neighbors as brothers and sisters. No other commandments are greater than these.[6] And we should ever revere the worth of human life, through each of its many stages.

Scripture teaches that the body and the spirit are the soul of man.[7] As a dual being, each of you can thank God for His priceless gifts of your body and your spirit.

My professional years as a medical doctor gave me a profound respect for the human body. Created by God as a gift to you, it is absolutely amazing! Think of your eyes that see, ears that hear, and fingers that feel all the wondrous things around you. Your brain lets you learn, think, and reason. Your heart pumps tirelessly day and night, almost without your awareness.

Other God-given mechanisms are also at work in your body. Elements like sodium, potassium, and calcium and compounds like water, glucose, and proteins are essential for survival. The body deals with gases like oxygen and carbon dioxide. It makes hormones like insulin, adrenalin, and thyroxin. Levels of each of these and many other constituents in the body are auto-regulated within certain bounds.

Servo-regulatory relationships exist between glands of the body. For example, the pituitary gland at the base of the brain emits a hormone to stimulate the cortex of the adrenal glands to produce adrenal cortical hormones. Rising levels of cortical hormones in turn suppress the pituitary's output of the stimulating hormone and vice versa. Your body temperature is maintained at a normal range of 98.6°F or 37°C, whether you're at the equator or at the North Pole.

With your body being such a vital part of God's eternal plan, it is little wonder that the Apostle Paul described it as a "temple of God."[8] Each time you look in the mirror, see your body as your temple. That truth—refreshed gratefully each day—can positively influence your decisions about how you will care for your body and how you will use it. And those decisions will determine your destiny. How could this be? Because your body is the temple for your spirit. And how you use your body affects your spirit. Some of the decisions that will determine your eternal destiny include:

How will you choose to care for and use your body?

What spiritual attributes will you choose to develop?

Your spirit is an eternal entity. The Lord said to His prophet Abraham: "Thou wast chosen before thou wast born."[9] The Lord said something similar about Jeremiah[10] and many others.[11] He even said it about you.[12]

Your Heavenly Father has known you for a very long time.

You, as His son or daughter, were chosen by Him to come to earth at this precise time, to be a leader in His great work on earth.[13] You were chosen *not* for your bodily characteristics but for your *spiritual* attributes, such as bravery, courage, integrity of heart, a thirst for truth, a hunger for wisdom, and a desire to serve others.

You developed some of these attributes premortally. Others you can develop here on earth[14] as you persistently seek them.[15]

A pivotal spiritual attribute is that of self-mastery—the strength to place reason over appetite. Self-mastery builds a strong conscience. And your conscience determines your moral responses in difficult, tempting, and trying situations. Fasting helps your spirit to develop dominance over your physical appetites. Fasting also increases your access to heaven's help, as it intensifies your prayers.

Why the need for self-mastery? God implanted strong appetites within us for nourishment and love, vital for the human family to be perpetuated.[16] When we master our appetites within the bounds of God's laws, we can enjoy longer life, greater love, and consummate joy.[17]

It is not surprising, then, that most temptations to stray from God's plan of happiness come through the misuse of those essential, God-given appetites. Controlling our appetites is not always easy. Not one of us manages them perfectly.[18] Mistakes happen. Errors are made. Sins are committed. What can we do then? We can learn from them. And we can truly repent.[19]

We can change our behavior. Our very desires can change. How? There is only one way. True change—permanent change—can come only through the healing, cleansing, and enabling power of the Atonement of Jesus Christ.[20] He loves you![21] He allows you to access His power as you keep His commandments eagerly, earnestly, and exactly. It is that simple and certain. The gospel of Jesus Christ *is* a gospel of change![22]

A strong human spirit with control over appetites of the flesh is master over emotions and passions and not a slave to them. That kind of freedom is as vital to the spirit as oxygen is to the body! Freedom from self-slavery is true liberation![23]

We are "free to choose liberty and eternal life . . . or to choose captivity and death."[24] When we choose the loftier path toward liberty and eternal life, that path includes marriage.[25] Latter-day Saints proclaim that "marriage between a man and a woman is ordained of God and that the family is central to the Creator's plan for the eternal destiny of His children." We also know that "gender is an essential characteristic of individual premortal, mortal, and eternal identity and purpose."[26]

Marriage between a man and a woman is fundamental

to the Lord's doctrine and crucial to God's eternal plan. Marriage between a man and a woman is God's pattern for a fulness of life on earth and in heaven. God's marriage pattern cannot be abused, misunderstood, or misconstrued.[27] Not if you want true joy. God's marriage pattern protects the sacred power of procreation and the joy of true marital intimacy.[28] We know that Adam and Eve were married by God before they ever experienced the joy of uniting as husband and wife.[29]

In our day civil governments have a vested interest in protecting marriage because strong families constitute the best way of providing for the health, education, welfare, and prosperity of rising generations.[30] But civil governments are heavily influenced by social trends and secular philosophies as they write, rewrite, and enforce laws. Regardless of what civil legislation may be enacted, the doctrine of the Lord regarding marriage and morality *cannot be changed.*[31] Remember: sin, even if legalized by man, is still sin in the eyes of God!

While we are to emulate our Savior's kindness and compassion, while we are to value the rights and feelings of all of God's children, we cannot change His doctrine. It is not ours to change. His doctrine is ours to study, understand, and uphold.

The Savior's way of life is good. His way includes chastity

before marriage and total fidelity within marriage.[32] The Lord's way is the only way for us to experience enduring happiness. His way brings sustained comfort to our souls and perennial peace to our homes. And best of all, His way leads us home to Him and our Heavenly Father, to eternal life and exaltation.[33] This is the very essence of God's work and glory.[34]

Yes, each day is a day of decision, and our decisions determine our destiny. One day each of us will stand before the Lord in judgment.[35] We will each have a personal interview with Jesus Christ.[36] We will account for decisions that we made about our bodies, our spiritual attributes, and how we honored God's pattern for marriage and family. May we choose wisely each day's decisions for eternity.

There is only One
in whom your faith is always safe,
and that is
THE LORD JESUS CHRIST.

CHAPTER 8

WE CAN ACT IN FAITH

On a recent flight, our pilot announced that we would encounter turbulence during our descent and that all passengers must fasten their seat belts securely. Sure enough, turbulence came. It was really rough. Across the aisle and a couple of rows behind me, a terrified woman panicked. With each frightening drop and jarring bump, she screamed loudly. Her husband tried to comfort her, but to no avail. Her hysterical shouts persisted until we passed through that zone of turbulence to a safe landing. During her period of anxiety, I felt sorry for her. Because faith is the antidote for fear, I silently wished that I could have strengthened her faith.

Later, as passengers were leaving the aircraft, this woman's husband spoke to me. He said, "I'm sorry my wife was so terrified. The only way I could comfort her was to tell her, 'Elder Nelson is on this flight, so you don't need to worry.'"

I'm not sure that my presence on that flight should have given her any comfort, but I will say that one of the realities of mortal life is that our faith will be tested and challenged. Sometimes those tests come as we face what appear to be life-and-death encounters. For this frightened woman, a violently rocking plane presented one of those moments when we come face-to-face with the strength of our faith.

When we speak of faith—the faith that can move mountains—we are not speaking of faith in general, but of faith in the Lord Jesus Christ. Faith in the Lord Jesus Christ can be bolstered as we learn about Him and live our religion. The doctrine of Jesus Christ was designed by the Lord to help us increase our faith. In today's vernacular, however, the word *religion* can mean different things to different people.

The word *religion* literally means "to ligate again," or "to tie back" to God.[1] The question we might ask ourselves is, are we securely tied to God so that our faith shows, or are we actually tied to something else? For example, I have overheard conversations on Monday mornings about professional athletic games that took place on the preceding Sunday. For some of these avid fans, I have wondered if their "religion" would "tie them back" only to some kind of a bouncing ball.

We might each ask ourselves, where is our faith? Is it in

a team? Is it in a brand? Is it in a celebrity? Even the best teams can fail. Celebrities can fade. There is only One in whom your faith is always safe, and that is the Lord Jesus Christ. And you need to let your faith show!

God declared in the *first* of His Ten Commandments, "Thou shalt have no other gods before me."[2] He also said, "Look unto me in every thought; doubt not, fear not."[3] Yet so many people look only to their bank balance for peace, or to fellow human beings for models to follow.

Clinicians, academicians, and politicians are often put to a test of faith. In pursuit of their goals, will their religion show or will it be hidden? Are they tied back to God or to man?

I had such a test decades ago when one of my medical faculty colleagues chastised me for failing to separate my professional knowledge from my religious convictions. He demanded that I *not* combine the two. How could I keep from doing that? Truth is truth! It is not divisible; no part of it can be set aside.

Whether truth emerges from a scientific laboratory or through revelation, all truth emanates from God. All truth is part of the gospel of Jesus Christ.[4] Yet, I was being asked to hide my faith. I did not comply with my colleague's request. I let my faith show!

In all professional endeavors, rigorous standards of

accuracy are required. Scholars cherish their freedom of expression. But full freedom cannot be experienced if part of one's knowledge is ruled "out of bounds" by edicts of men.

Spiritual truth cannot be ignored—especially divine commandments. Keeping divine commandments brings blessings,[5] every time! Breaking divine commandments brings a loss of blessings, every time!

Problems abound in this world because it is populated by imperfect people. Their objectives and desires are heavily influenced by their faith, or lack of it. Many put other priorities ahead of God. Some challenge the relevance of religion in modern life. As in every age, so today there are those who mock or decry the free exercise of religion. Some even blame religion for any number of the world's ills. Admittedly, there have been times when atrocities have been committed in the name of religion. But living the Lord's pure religion, which means striving to become a true disciple of Jesus Christ, is a way of life and a daily commitment that will provide divine guidance. As you practice your religion, you are exercising your faith. You are letting your faith show.

The Lord knew that His children would need to learn how to find Him. "For strait is the gate," He said, "and narrow the way that leadeth unto . . . exaltation . . . and few there be that find it."[6]

The scriptures provide one of the best ways to find our

course and stay on it. Scriptural knowledge also provides precious protection. For example, throughout history, infections like "childbirth fever" claimed the lives of many innocent mothers and babies. Yet, the Old Testament, written more than three thousand years ago, had the correct principles for the handling of infected patients![7] Many people perished because man's quest for knowledge had failed to heed the word of the Lord!

What are we missing in our lives if we are "ever learning, [but] never able to come to the knowledge of the truth?"[8] We can gain great knowledge from the scriptures and obtain inspiration through prayers of faith.

Doing so will help us as we make daily decisions. Especially when the laws of man are created and enforced, God's laws must ever be our standard. In dealing with controversial issues, we should first search for God's guidance.

We should "liken all scriptures unto us, . . . for our profit and learning."[9] Danger lurks when we try to divide ourselves with expressions such as "my private life" or even "my best behavior." If one tries to segment his or her life into such separate compartments, one will never rise to the full stature of one's personal integrity—never to become all that his or her *true* self could be.

The temptation to be popular may prioritize public opinion above the word of God. Political campaigns and marketing strategies widely employ public opinion polls to shape their plans. Results of those polls are informative, *but* they could hardly be used as grounds to justify disobedience to God's commandments! Even if "everyone is doing it," wrong is never right. Evil, error, and darkness will never be truth, even if popular. A scriptural warning so declares: "Woe unto them that call evil good, and good evil; that put darkness for light, and light for darkness."[10]

After World War I, a rather risqué song became popular. In promoting immorality, it vowed that fifty million people cannot be wrong. But in fact, fifty million people *can* be wrong—totally wrong. Immorality is still immorality in the eyes of God, who one day will judge all of our deeds and desires.[11]

Contrast the fear and faithlessness so prevalent in the world today with the faith and courage of my dearly beloved daughter Emily, who now lives on the other side of the veil. As mortal life was leaving her cancer-ridden body, she could barely speak. But with a smile on her face, she said to me, "Daddy, don't worry about me. I know I will be all right!" Emily's faith was showing—showing brightly—in that tender moment, right when we needed it most.

This beautiful young mother of five had full faith in her Heavenly Father, in His plan, and in the eternal welfare of her family. She was securely tied back to God. She was totally faithful to covenants made with the Lord and with her husband. She loved her children, but was at peace despite her impending separation from them. She had faith in her future, and theirs, too, because she had faith in our Heavenly Father and His Son.

President Thomas S. Monson has said: "Of course we will face fear, experience ridicule, and meet opposition. Let us have the courage to defy the consensus, the courage to stand for principle. Courage, not compromise, brings the smile of God's approval. . . . Remember that all men have their fears, but those who face their fears with [faith] have courage as well."[12]

President Monson's counsel is timeless! So I plead with you: Day after day, on your path toward your eternal destiny, increase your faith. Proclaim your faith! Let your faith show![13]

I pray that you will be securely tied back to God, that His eternal truths will be etched on your heart forever. And I pray that, throughout your life, you will let your faith show!

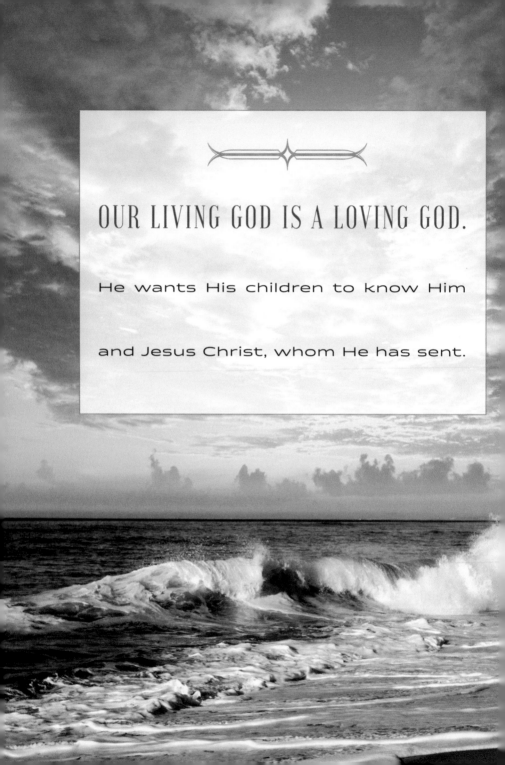

OUR LIVING GOD IS A LOVING GOD.

He wants His children to know Him

and Jesus Christ, whom He has sent.

CHAPTER 9

WE CAN SHARE THE GOSPEL

From time to time we need to remind ourselves that we are a Church with a missionary mandate. This is because of a commandment from the Lord, who said, "Go ye therefore, and teach all nations, baptizing them in the name of the Father, and of the Son, and of the Holy Ghost: Teaching them to observe all things whatsoever I have commanded you: and, lo, I am with you alway, even unto the end of the world."[1]

This commandment is one of many that have been renewed because the gospel of Jesus Christ has been restored in its fulness. Missionaries serve now just as they did in New Testament times. The book of Acts describes early missionary labors of the Apostles and other disciples following the Lord's mortal ministry. There we read of the remarkable conversion and baptism of Saul of Tarsus,[2] who had previously been "breathing out threatenings and slaughter against the disciples of the Lord"[3] and persecuting members of the fledgling Church. From such beginnings, Saul became the converted Paul, one of the Lord's greatest missionaries. The final fifteen chapters of the book of Acts report the missionary labors of Paul and his companions.

In a letter to one of his most trusted companions, Paul wrote to young Timothy, "Let no man despise thy youth; but *be thou an example of the believers,* in word, in conversation, in charity, in spirit, in faith, in purity."[4] That counsel is just as valid for us now as it was then. It applies to our full-time missionaries; it applies equally to each member of the Church. Whether full-time missionaries or members, we should all be good examples of the believers in Jesus Christ.

Full-time missionaries are believers and devoted servants of the Lord. Their purpose is to "invite others to come unto Christ by helping them receive the restored gospel through faith in Jesus Christ and His Atonement, repentance, baptism, receiving the gift of the Holy Ghost, and enduring to the end."[5]

Missionaries serve to make life better for God's children. Heavenly Father loves every one of His children. After all, He is their Father. He wants to bless them with His greatest gift, that of eternal life.[6] Missionaries so teach wherever they serve. They help people to develop faith in the Lord, repent, be baptized, receive the Holy Ghost, receive the ordinances of the temple, and endure faithfully to the end. God's work and glory—"to bring to pass the immortality and eternal life of man,"[7]—is also the sacred work and glory of each missionary.

We need more missionaries—more worthy missionaries. During His earthly ministry the Lord told His disciples, "The harvest truly is great, but the labourers are few: pray ye therefore the Lord of the harvest, that he would send forth labourers into his harvest."[8]

Since President Thomas S. Monson's historic announcement lowering the age of eligibility for missionary service,[9] an unprecedented wave of enthusiasm for missionary work has been sweeping the entire earth. Thousands of elders, sisters, and couples have been called, and many more are preparing. Now we get questions like "What are you going to do with all these missionaries?" The answer is simple. They will do what missionaries have always done. They will preach the gospel! They will bless the children of Almighty God!

More of you young men and women will catch this wave as you strive to be worthy of mission calls. You see this as a wave of truth and righteousness. You see your opportunity to be on the crest of that wave.

You teenagers, embrace your new curriculum and teach

one another the doctrine of Jesus Christ. Now is your time to prepare to teach others about the goodness of God.

You adults, catch the wave with help for the spiritual, physical, and financial preparation of future missionaries. Pinching pennies for piggy banks becomes part of your practice. You senior couples, you plan for the day when you can go on your mission. We will be most grateful for your service. Until then, perhaps you could send your dollars on missions by contributing to the General Missionary Fund.

Our inquiring friends and neighbors not of our faith can also catch the wave. We encourage them to keep all that is good and true in their lives. And we invite them to receive more, especially the glorious truth that through God's eternal plan, families can be together forever.[10]

This wave of truth and righteousness is wondrous! It is *not* man-made! It comes from the Lord, who said, "I will hasten my work in its time."[11] This wave is empowered by a divine announcement made nearly two hundred years ago. It consisted of only seven words: *"This is My Beloved Son. Hear Him!"*[12] Uttered by Almighty God, that announcement introduced a young Joseph Smith to the Lord Jesus Christ. Those seven words launched the Restoration of His gospel. Why? Because our living God is a loving God! He wants His children to know Him and Jesus Christ, whom He has sent![13]

And He wants His children to gain immortality and eternal life![14]

As He loves us, it is our responsibility to share that love with all His children. To illustrate how our Heavenly Father expects us to love one another, I will share with you a parable that I call "A Father at Bedtime."

A caring father is seated at home one evening after his wife and children have gone to bed. He feels an impulse—a prompting—to check on the children. He takes off his shoes and walks quietly to the door of a bedroom. In the dim light from an open doorway, he sees two little heads on pillows, and blankets covering these snuggling children, soundly sleeping.

As he listens to their quiet breathing, his mind rehearses scenes from earlier in the day. He hears their laughter as they played together. He sees their smiles as they shared a picnic, and their giggles when they were caught feeding ice cream to the dog. (Patience with children comes more easily when they are asleep.) As they slumber, he ponders what they need and how he can help them. He feels a surge of love and a strong duty to protect them.

He tiptoes to a second bedroom, where two older children should be. He sees two beds, but his heart skips a beat when he finds that one of those beds is empty.

He spins around and walks to the study, where he has on

occasion found this missing daughter. There he finds her in a chair, quietly reading a book.

"I couldn't sleep," she says.

He pulls up a chair next to her. They talk about her day, about her friends, about her goals and dreams. Later she returns to bed, and the father makes one final round before turning out the lights and retiring to his bed.

In the morning, the father assists his dear wife as she prepares breakfast. He sets a place for each of their children, even for the youngest, who likes to sleep longer. Aromas from the kitchen arouse the children and they come running in a blur of motion and chatter.

But one of the chairs is empty. The father asks them to wait while he goes to awaken the missing child. Soon, the entire family is together enjoying their breakfast.

What can we learn from this simple parable? The father followed his impulse to check on his children. He evaluated his relationship with them. He searched for a missing child. His actions were all motivated purely by love. He didn't do what he did because he had read a handbook. No one gave him a checklist. He followed the feelings of his heart.

So it is with missionary work. The most effective missionaries always act out of love. Love is the lubricant and life of good missionary work.

The father in the parable loved each child. So we, too,

should act out of love to help all, not just a favored few. Our example needs to shine for all to see.

Each one of us can be an example of the believers. As followers of Jesus Christ, we can live in accord with His teachings. We can have "the image of God engraven upon [our countenance]."[15] Our good works will be evident to others.[16] The light of the Lord can beam from our eyes.[17] With that radiance, we had better prepare for questions. The Apostle Peter so counseled: "Be ready always to give an answer to every man that asketh you a reason of the hope that is in you."[18]

Let your response be warm and joyful. And let your response be relevant to that individual. Remember, he or she is also a child of God, that very God who dearly wants that person to qualify for eternal life and return to Him one day. You may be the very one to open the door to his or her salvation and understanding of the doctrine of Christ.[19]

As that door begins to open, remain mindful of the unchanging principle that lies at the foundation of all we do in missionary work, and that is that the Holy Ghost is the true teacher. Spiritual communication and true conversion are accomplished through the power of the Holy Ghost.

In order for us to teach anything, we must be attuned to the Spirit of the Lord. Perhaps I could demonstrate what I mean by "being attuned" with an analogy of tuning forks. If

I have two tuning forks tuned to the same frequency, I can make an interesting thing happen. When I tap the first fork, tuned to, say, middle C on the piano, it makes the sound of middle C.

Now, if I hold the second fork close to the first one, and tap the first one again, both forks make the sound of middle C! This works because they are tuned to the same frequency. Whether the first tone comes from a tuning fork or another source, either fork will respond to a middle C. If I played that note on the piano, both tuning forks would sing.

Imagine now a third tuning fork, tuned just a half step below middle C. I can tap the first fork and hold it close to this third fork, and nothing will happen. The fork tuned to the B will not respond because it is tuned to a different frequency.

If the Spirit of the Lord comes at its own unique frequency, you will resonate to it if you are in tune with it. But if your frequency is different, you will not respond or resonate with that same Spirit.

This physical law is suggested in the statement of the Lord, "My sheep hear my voice, and I know them, and they follow me."[20]

Now, tuning forks cannot change their frequency, but people can. They can become in tune with the Spirit. We can also become attuned to people when we are trying to teach them the gospel. We can strive to find common ground. If we can understand what is on our friend's mind, if we can become spiritually connected, if we can be compassionate and sympathetic to the trials faced by our friend, then we will be in tune with each other.

Once you feel that resonance operating, be ready to take the next step. You may invite your friend to attend church with you. Many of our friends do not know they are welcome in our church buildings. "Come and see" was the Savior's invitation to those who desired to learn more about Him.[21] An invitation to attend a Sunday meeting with you, or to participate in a Church social or service activity, will help to dispel mistaken myths and make visitors feel more comfortable among us.

As a member of the Church, reach out to those you do not know, and greet them warmly. Each Sunday extend a hand of fellowship to at least one person you did not know before. Each day of your life, strive to enlarge your own circle of friendship.

You can invite a friend to read the Book of Mormon. Explain that it is not a novel or a history book. It is another testament of Jesus Christ. Its very purpose is "to the convincing of the Jew and Gentile that Jesus is the Christ, the Eternal God, manifesting himself unto all nations."[22] There is a power in this book that can touch the hearts and lift the lives of honest seekers of truth. Invite your friend to read the book prayerfully.

The Prophet Joseph Smith said "that the Book of Mormon was the most correct of any book on earth, and the keystone of our religion, and a man would get nearer to God by abiding by its precepts, than by any other book."[23] The Book of Mormon teaches of the Atonement of Jesus Christ and is the instrument by which God will fulfill His ancient promise to gather scattered Israel in these latter days.[24]

Many years ago, two colleagues of mine—a nurse and her doctor husband—asked me why I lived the way I did. I answered, "Because I know the Book of Mormon is true." I let them borrow my copy of the book, inviting them to read it. A week later they returned my book with a polite "thanks a lot."

I responded, "What do you mean, thanks a lot? That's a totally inappropriate response for one who has read this book. You didn't read it, did you? Please take it back and read it; then I would like my book back."

Admitting that they had only turned its pages, they accepted my invitation. When they returned they said tearfully, "We have read the Book of Mormon. We know it is true! We want to know more." They learned more, and it was my privilege to baptize both of them.

Another way that you can share the gospel is to invite

friends to meet with full-time missionaries in your home. Those missionaries are called and prepared to teach the gospel. Your friends, in the comfort of your home and with your constant reassurance, can begin their journey toward salvation and exaltation. The Lord said, "Ye are called to bring to pass the gathering of mine elect; for mine elect hear my voice and harden not their hearts."[25]

Scripture tells us that "there are many yet on the earth . . . who are only kept from the truth because they know not where to find it."[26] Isn't that your opportunity? You can become their own disciple of discovery!

Now, in this day of the Internet, there are new and exciting ways you can do missionary work. You can invite friends and neighbors to visit the mormon.org website. If you have blogs and online social networks, you could link your sites to mormon.org. And there you can create your own personal profile. Each profile includes an expression of belief, an experience, and a testimony.

These profiles can have a profound influence for good. Just one example: a young man saw an ad for mormon.org on television in his hometown. He connected with the website and was intrigued by the profiles of Church members. At our website he found the link that informed him where he could attend church. The next Sunday, dressed in a white shirt and tie, he attended church, was introduced to members of the ward, and enjoyed all three hours of meetings. He was invited to a member's home for dinner, followed by his first missionary lesson. In less than two weeks, he was baptized and confirmed as a member of the Church.[27]

Each exemplary follower of Jesus Christ can become an effective member missionary. Members and full-time missionaries may walk arm in arm in bringing the blessings of the gospel to cherished friends and neighbors. Many of them are of Israel, now being gathered as promised. This is all part of the preparation for the Second Coming of the Lord.[28] He wants each of us truly to be an example of the believers.

of our members must become

the primary sanctuaries of our

FAITH,

where each can be safe

FROM THE SINS OF THE WORLD.

CHAPTER 10

WE CAN STRENGTHEN OUR FAMILIES

In the Church, we stress the significance of marriage, children, and the family because we know the doctrine. And we know that the adversary incessantly aims attacks at the family. In the past fifty years the birthrate has dropped in nearly every nation of the world. Marriages are being postponed until later in life, and families are getting smaller, even in the Church.

While the family is under attack throughout the world, The Church of Jesus Christ of Latter-day Saints proclaims, promotes, and protects the truth that the family is central to the Creator's plan for the eternal destiny of His children. "The Family—A Proclamation to the World" and our vast family history efforts are but two evidences of how this Church brings hope and help to the sacred institution of the family.

Our task to defend the family is not an easy one. Trends in the world diminish the significance of the family. Sadly, the sacred powers of procreation are desecrated by many people. And the divinely designed nature of marital intimacy is tarnished by the addictive, pernicious, and poisonous plague of pornography.

In reality, we are raising our children in enemy-occupied territory. The homes of our members must become the primary sanctuaries of our faith, where each can be safe from the sins of the world.

Our Master depends upon us to live according to His truth. Marriage is ordained of God. It is doctrinally based and eternally significant. The Lord has taught:

"From the beginning of the creation God made them male and female.

"For this cause shall a man leave his father and mother, and *cleave* to his wife;

"And they twain shall be one flesh."[1]

Three times in sacred scripture the warning is made that "the whole earth would be utterly wasted" at the Lord's return if certain conditions were not in place.[2] In each instance that warning relates to the condition of the human family without the sealing ordinances of the temple. Without these ordinances of exaltation, the glory of God would not be realized.[3]

Because of the Atonement, the consummate blessings associated with these ordinances can be realized by each of God's children who obeys His eternal laws. Through the ages, many of His children have had access to the blessings of the gospel, but many more have not. Before the foundation of the world, our Heavenly Father instituted the ordinance of baptism for the dead for those who die without a knowledge of the gospel.[4] He loves those children, too.

He also provided a way for them to be part of an eternal family. Every human being who comes to this earth is the product of generations of parents. We have a natural yearning to connect with our ancestors. This desire dwells in our hearts, regardless of age.

Consider the spiritual connections that are formed when a young woman helps her grandmother enter family information into a computer, or when a young man sees the name of his great-grandfather on a census record. When our hearts turn to our ancestors, something changes inside us. We feel part of something greater than ourselves. Our inborn yearnings for family connections are fulfilled when we are linked to our ancestors through sacred ordinances of the temple.

While temple and family history work has the power to bless those beyond the veil, it has an equal power to bless the living. It has a refining influence on those who are engaged in it. They are literally helping to exalt their families.

We are exalted when we can dwell together with our extended families in the presence of Almighty God. The Prophet Joseph Smith foresaw our duty: "The great day of the Lord is at hand," he said. "Let us, therefore, as a church and a people, and as Latter-day Saints, offer unto the Lord an offering in righteousness; and let us present in his holy temple . . . a book containing the records of our dead, which shall be worthy of all acceptation."[5]

The preparation of that record is our individual and collective responsibility. As we work together, we can make it worthy of all acceptation by the Lord. That record enables ordinances to be performed for and accepted by our deceased ancestors, as they may choose. Those ordinances can bring liberty to captives on the other side of the veil.[6]

Family relationships that stretch for eternity start with the love of a husband for his wife, and of a wife for her husband. Marriage brings two very different and imperfect people together. Husbands and wives deal with their imperfections best with patience and a sense of humor. Each should stand ready to say, "I'm sorry! Please forgive me." And each should be a peacemaker.

Each personal imperfection is an opportunity to change—to repent. Repentance, at any age, provides needed progress. You repent with a mighty change of heart, which leads to a love of God and your neighbor, especially that neighbor to whom you are married. Repentance includes forgiveness, and forgiveness is a commandment. The Lord said, "I . . . will forgive whom I will forgive, but of you it is required to forgive all men."[7] When repentance is complete, you even forgive yourself.

Differences of opinion may occur between husband and wife. But one's objective in marriage is never to win an argument, but to build an eternal relationship of love.

Marriage is sanctified by family prayer morning and night, and daily scripture study. Marriage is stabilized by careful financial planning, avoiding debt, and living within a budget with willing obedience to the Lord's law of tithing. Marriage is energized by making prime time together. Marriage is protected by an absolute commitment to make it successful.

Each married bearer of the priesthood needs to remember that his highest duty is to care for his wife. She enables him to qualify for his greatest blessings. And when the children leave the nest, a husband and his wife will have each other in what can be a wonderful and exciting phase of life together.

Parenting is a joint venture. The father exercises his leadership with light and love, never in any degree of unrighteousness.[8] The mother provides the intuition, the inspiration, and the nurture that come from her so naturally.

Together they obey the Lord's commandment to teach the gospel to their children.[9] Jesus wants children to come unto Him, "for of such is the kingdom of heaven."[10] Parents are responsible for that teaching, with assistance from the Church. All that the future holds in store for each sacred child of God will be shaped by his or her parents, family, friends, and teachers. Thus, our faith *now* becomes part of our posterity's faith *later.*

Each individual will make his or her way in a constantly changing world—a world of competing ideologies. The forces of evil will ever be in opposition to the forces of good. Satan constantly strives to influence us to follow his ways and make us miserable, even as he is.[11] And the normal risks of life such as illness, injury, and accident will ever be present.

We live in a time of turmoil. Earthquakes and tsunamis wreak devastation, governments collapse, economic stresses are severe, the family is under attack, and divorce rates are rising. We have great cause for concern. But we do not need to let our fears displace our faith. We can combat those fears by strengthening our faith.

Start with your children. You parents bear the primary responsibility to strengthen their faith. Let them feel your faith, even when sore trials come upon you. Let your faith be focused on our loving Heavenly Father and His Beloved Son, the Lord Jesus Christ. Teach that faith with deep conviction.

Teach each precious boy or girl that he or she is a child of God, created in His image, with a sacred purpose and potential. Each is born with challenges to overcome and faith to be developed.[12]

Teach of faith in God's plan of salvation. Teach that our sojourn in mortality is a period of probation, a time of trial and testing to see if we will do whatever the Lord commands us to do.[13]

Teach of faith to keep *all* the commandments of God, knowing that they are given to bless His children and bring them joy.[14] Warn your children that they will encounter people who pick which commandments they will keep and ignore others that they choose to break. I call this the "cafeteria" approach to obedience. This practice of picking and choosing will not work. It will lead to misery. To prepare to meet God, one keeps *all* of His commandments. It takes faith to obey them, and keeping His commandments will strengthen that faith.

Obedience allows God's blessings to flow without constraint. He will bless His obedient children with freedom from bondage and misery. And He will bless them with more light. For example, one keeps the Word of Wisdom knowing that obedience will not only bring freedom from addiction, but it will also add blessings of wisdom and treasures of knowledge.[15]

Teach of faith to know that obedience to the commandments of God will provide physical and spiritual protection. And remember, God's holy angels are ever on call to help us. The Lord so declared: "I will go before your face. I will be on your right hand and on your left, and my Spirit shall be in your hearts, and mine angels round about you, to bear you up."[16] What a promise! When we are faithful, He and His angels will help us.

Unfailing faith is fortified through prayer. Your heartfelt pleadings are important to Him. Think of the intense and impassioned prayers of the Prophet Joseph Smith during his dreadful days of incarceration in Liberty Jail. The Lord responded by changing the Prophet's perspective. He said, "Know thou, my son, that all these things shall give thee experience, and shall be for thy good."[17]

If we pray with an eternal perspective, we need not wonder if our most tearful and heartfelt pleadings are heard. This promise from the Lord is recorded in section 98 of the Doctrine and Covenants: "Your prayers have entered into the ears of the Lord . . . and are recorded with this seal and testament—the Lord hath sworn and decreed that they shall be granted.

"Therefore, he giveth this promise unto you, with an immutable covenant that they shall be fulfilled; and all things wherewith you have been afflicted shall work together for your good, and to my name's glory, saith the Lord."[18]

The Lord chose His strongest words to reassure us! *Seal! Testament! Sworn! Decreed! Immutable covenant!* Believe Him! God will heed your sincere and heartfelt prayers, and your faith will be strengthened.

To develop enduring faith, an enduring commitment to be a full-tithe payer is essential. Initially it takes faith to tithe. Then the tithe payer develops more faith, to the point that tithing becomes a precious privilege. Tithing is an ancient law from God.[19] He made a promise to His children that He would open "the windows of heaven, and pour . . . out a blessing, that there shall not be room enough to receive it."[20] Not only that, tithing will keep your name enrolled among the people of God and protect you in "the day of vengeance and burning."[21]

Why do we need such resilient faith? Because difficult days are ahead. Rarely in the future will it be easy or popular to be a faithful Latter-day Saint. Each of us will be tested. The Apostle Paul warned that in the latter days, those who diligently follow the Lord "shall suffer persecution."[22] That very persecution can either crush you into silent weakness or motivate you to be more exemplary and courageous in your daily life.

How you deal with life's trials is part of the development of your faith. Strength comes when you remember that you have a divine nature, an inheritance of infinite worth. The Lord has reminded you, your children, and your grandchildren that you are lawful heirs, that you have been reserved in heaven for your specific time and place to be born, to grow and become His standard bearers and covenant people. As you walk in the Lord's path of righteousness, you will be blessed to continue in His goodness and be a light and a savior unto His people.[23]

Available to both brethren and sisters are blessings obtained through the power of the holy Melchizedek Priesthood. These blessings can change the circumstances of your life in matters such as health, companionship of the Holy Ghost, personal relationships, and opportunities for the future. The power and authority of this priesthood holds "the keys of all the spiritual blessings of the Church."[24] And, most remarkably, the Lord has declared that He will sustain those blessings, according to His will.[25]

The greatest of all the blessings of the priesthood are bestowed in holy temples of the Lord. Fidelity to covenants made there will qualify you and your family for the blessings of eternal life.[26]

Your rewards come not only hereafter. Many blessings will be yours in this life, among your children and grandchildren. If you are faithful, you do not have to fight life's battles alone. Think of that! The Lord declared, "I will contend with him that contendeth with thee, and I will save thy children."[27] Later came this promise to His faithful people: "I, the Lord, would fight their battles, and their children's battles, and their children's children's, . . . to the third and fourth generation."[28]

Our beloved President Thomas S. Monson has given us his prophetic witness. He said, "I testify to you that our promised blessings are beyond measure. Though the storm clouds may gather, though the rains may pour down upon us, our knowledge of the gospel and our love of our Heavenly Father and of our Savior will comfort and sustain us and bring joy to our hearts as we walk uprightly and keep the commandments."

President Monson continued, "My beloved brothers and sisters, fear not. Be of good cheer. The future is as bright as your faith."[29]

God's plan of happiness is perfect. As we teach it in our families, we bless all with love, hope, peace, and joy, here and hereafter.

Through the blessings, ordinances,

and covenants of the temple,

families

CAN BE TOGETHER

FOREVER.

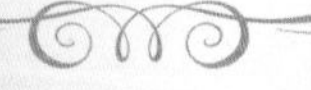

CHAPTER 11

WE CAN MAKE RIGHTEOUS CHOICES

As members of The Church of Jesus Christ of Latter-day Saints, we are all partakers of a noble birthright. We are literally sons and daughters of God, born at this particular time in the world's history for a most sacred purpose. Although the moral and religious values of society seem to be weakening across the globe, members of *this* Church are to be standard bearers of the Lord, beacons of light to attract others to Him. Your identity and purpose are unique.

What is your identity? You are children of the covenant. What covenant? That which God made with father Abraham, when Abraham was promised that "in thy seed shall all the kindreds of the earth be blessed."[1] You are also children of the promised day,[2] this period of world history when the gospel will be broadly proclaimed across this planet.

Each one of you was commissioned by your Heavenly

Father to build up the kingdom of God on earth right now and to prepare a people to receive the Savior when He will rule and reign as the Millennial Messiah. Your noble birthright, identity, purpose, and divine commission set you apart from all others.

But neither your birthright nor your premortal ordinations and commissions can save or exalt you. That you will do through your individual decisions and as you choose to access the power of the Lord's Atonement in your lives. You know that "every soul is free to choose his life and what he'll be."[3] That great, eternal principle of agency is vital to our Father's plan. So, you of the noble birthright, what will you choose?

Will you choose to increase in learning?

Education is yours to obtain. No one else can gain it for you. Wherever you are, develop a deep desire to learn. For us as Latter-day Saints, getting an education is not just a privilege, it is a religious responsibility. "The glory of God is intelligence."[4] Indeed, our education is for the eternities.

"Whatever principle of intelligence we attain unto in this life, it will rise with us in the resurrection.

"And if a person gains more knowledge and intelligence in this life . . . he [or she] will have so much the advantage in the world to come."[5]

Such a long-range perspective will help you make good

choices about learning. I remember a conversation many years ago with a very bright sixteen-year-old high school student. He was uncertain about his religious commitment and undecided about his career. He wondered about the possibility of becoming a doctor of medicine. He asked me a simple question: "How many years did it take for you to become a heart surgeon?"

I quickly made the calculations: "From the time I graduated from high school until I first collected a fee for service as a surgeon, it took me fourteen years!"

"Wow!" he replied. "That's too long for me!"

Then I asked, "How old will you be fourteen years from now if you *don't* become a heart surgeon?"

"Just the same," he replied, "just the same!"

I had a special interest in this young man. On occasion, I took him in my car on his early-morning route to deliver newspapers. Over the years, his faith became strong. He was a powerful missionary. He decided to pursue his educational goal. First, he married his sweetheart. Then, while he studied medicine and surgery, they became parents of four wonderful children. Now he is fully board-certified as a heart surgeon—after intensive education and training over a period of fourteen years!

Don't be afraid to pursue your goals—even your dreams! There is no shortcut to excellence and competence.

Education is the difference between *wishing* you could help other people and being *able* to help them.

When you started out on your path of learning, you likely became accustomed to doing your tasks one by one. You enrolled for instruction; you passed your examinations; you jumped over high hurdles of expectation for you, as imposed by other people. But eventually, your effort to *do* tasks may be less meaningful than your effort to become who you can *be*.

You will have goals that are great, greater, and greatest. Great goals I relate to temporal attainment. You will continue to set great goals for yourself and achieve them one by one.

Greater goals I relate to developing your attributes of character. Attributes of character are worthy of our attention as we strive to become whom we ought to be.

Heading the list of greater goals would be the attribute of love, including its related qualities of kindness, compassion, courtesy, civility, and mercy. Fostered first in the family, love is centered at home. The most important work you will ever do is within the walls of your own home.

Gratitude is another greater goal. We have much for which we should be thankful. Serving many years as a cardiac surgeon, I developed a deep sense of gratitude for my heart, and for yours. Each organ of the body is truly remarkable. Even though our bodies come in all shapes and sizes, our broken bones can mend and become strong once again.

Skin lacerations can heal. A leak in the circulation can seal itself.

Gratefully we acknowledge that, as children of a loving Father in Heaven, our inheritance is sacred and our potential is infinite. Gratitude for our countless blessings is a greater goal.

Integrity is another greater goal. Integrity includes virtue, cleanliness, and honesty. In our world, there is so much of deceit. We learn of cheating in the classrooms, cheating in business, cheating in marriage, and so on. Even though these acts may not be discovered by others, the soul of a cheater suffers. Self-respect vanishes, conscience is warped, and character crumbles.

If education is a great goal, a greater goal would be wisdom. One can attain education without knowledge and knowledge without wisdom. The Old Testament reminds us that "all the earth sought to Solomon, to hear his wisdom, which God had put in his heart."[6] Such wisdom comes to you who know and apply the principles and eternal doctrine of Jesus Christ in your daily lives.

Wisdom includes attention to prophetic warnings. Today's prophets warn that pornography, infidelity, and immorality are all tools of the adversary. They will destroy you physically and spiritually. Satan's objective is to hook you and make you miserable, even as he is.[7] Shun these traps now and your future will be brighter.

Other greater goals include "faith, virtue, knowledge, temperance, patience, brotherly kindness, godliness, charity, humility, [and] diligence,"[8] all of which are attainable attributes, exemplified by the Lord.

One goal, and one goal alone, should become your greatest goal. What is that? It is the goal of eternal life. That goal is God's goal. That goal is God's glory.[9] The Lord has decreed that "eternal life . . . is the greatest of all the gifts of God."[10] This gift is a conditional gift. One must qualify for it by keeping the commandments of God and enduring to the end. That end includes the endowment and sealing ordinances of the holy temple. Through the blessings, ordinances, and covenants of the temple, families can be together forever.[11]

So, as you pursue your great, greater, and greatest goals, what manner of living will you choose?

As a Saint of the noble birthright, you are expected to live differently than others. You know what Paul said to young Timothy: "Be thou an example of the believers, in word, in conversation, in charity, in spirit, in faith, in purity."[12] Choose to think and to act differently from those of the world. Choose to look different and see what an influence for good you will become. As Sister Ardeth G. Kapp once said, "You can't be a life-saver, if you look like all the other swimmers on the beach!"[13]

God's plan allows the adversary to tempt you so that you, now in this mortal world, can exercise your agency to choose good over evil, to choose to repent, and choose to come unto Jesus Christ and follow His example. What a huge responsibility and a huge trust!

Your freedom to choose is clearly explained in the Book of Mormon: "Men are free according to the flesh. . . . They are free to choose liberty and eternal life, . . . or to choose captivity and death, according to the captivity and power of the devil; for he seeketh that all men might be miserable like unto himself."[14] What will you choose?

Another verse reveals that "wickedness never was happiness."[15] Many have tried to challenge that truth, and they have failed every time!

Your freedom to act for yourself is so central to your eternal progress and happiness[16] that the adversary exerts extraordinary efforts to undermine it. Satan truly is an incorrigible insomniac. Chances are, you have already experienced that!

Here is another question: Will you establish priorities to help you make your choices in life?

Your choices will not all be between good and evil. Many will be choices between two good options. Not all truths are created equal. So you will need to establish priorities. In your pursuit of knowledge, know that *the very most* important truth you can learn comes from the Lord. In His intercessory prayer to His Father, the Savior Himself confirmed this. He said: "This is life eternal, that they might know thee the only true God, and Jesus Christ, whom thou hast sent."[17] Above everything else you are seeking to learn, seek to know God, your Heavenly Father, and His Son, Jesus Christ. Come to know Them and love Them as I do.

Another priority scripture has helped me throughout my life. It is: "Seek ye first to build up the kingdom of God, and to establish his righteousness, and all these things shall be added unto you."[18]

More than anything else in this world, you want to make choices that lead to the ultimate and glorious destiny of eternal life. That is God's greatest goal for you.[19]

Another question: With whom will you choose to associate?

As you move along life's journey, you will become acquainted with people who do *not* believe in God. Many of them have not yet found divine truth and don't know where to look for it. You could be of help to them there. But as you mingle with nonbelievers, be aware that a few may not have your best interest at heart.[20] As soon as you discern that, flee from them quickly and permanently.[21]

Sadly, you will meet people whose desperate search for

something that seems to them like happiness takes them down the slippery slopes of sin. Beware of that slimy slide! Any pleasure in sin is only fleeting, and its haunting memories are smeared by gnawing and grinding guilt. The sinful warping of the embrace divinely designed to unite husband and wife is but a hollow counterfeit. Each unlawful experience is stripped of deep meaning and sweet memory.

Next question: Will you choose freedom or bondage?

Godless forces are all around. You are literally living in "enemy-occupied territory."[22] A plague of poisonous pornography abounds. It ensnares *all* who yield to its insidious grasp.

This was foreseen by the Lord, who said, "And now I show unto you a mystery, a thing which is had in secret chambers, to bring to pass even your destruction in process of time, and ye knew it not."[23] He added a second warning: "And again, I say unto you that the enemy in the secret chambers seeketh your lives."[24]

Consider how many people, in how many secret chambers, are seeking to destroy your life and happiness, right now! I plead with you precious brothers and sisters to shun pornography absolutely. It is as destructive as leprosy, as addictive as meth, and as corrosive as lye.

Carnal temptation is not new. The Apostle Peter warned of this same snare when he wrote, "They allure through the lusts of the flesh, . . . those that were clean. . . .

"While they promise them liberty, they themselves are the servants of corruption: for of whom a man is overcome, of the same is he brought in bondage."[25]

Avoid that bondage, my beloved friends. If you are presently viewing pornography, *stop! Now!* Seek help from your bishop. None are smart enough to outwit the adversary on their own, once they have been poisoned by pornography.

Another reality is that you live at a time when unemployment is high and financial markets throughout the world are jittery. Again, a worldly solution is to look for alternatives to God's plan. But we know that strong marriages and families actually *help* the economy to *thrive*. And we are not alone in those feelings.

Dr. Patrick F. Fagan[26] wrote: "The indispensable building block upon which the fortunes of the economy depends is the married parent household—especially the child-rich family that worships weekly. Every marriage creates a new household, an independent economic unit that generates income, spends, saves, and invests."[27]

Dr. Fagan added that the "married mother at home exerts a more far-reaching impact on the economy than the married father in the workplace.

" . . . While the husband contributes to the present economy, the mother contributes to both present and future economy."[28]

Dr. Fagan's report confirms concepts expressed years ago by the First Presidency and the Twelve Apostles in "The Family—A Proclamation to the World." While the family is under attack across the entire world, the truths of the family proclamation will fortify you.

Now for a question I pray that you will consider on a daily basis: How will you prepare for your personal interview with the Savior?

You are not perfect. None of us are. So, you, along with the rest of us, are very grateful for the Atonement of the Savior, which provides full forgiveness as you truly repent. You also know that your stay here in mortality is relatively brief. (The older one gets, the more evident this fact becomes.) In time, each of us will one day graduate from this frail existence and move on to the next world.

Judgment day awaits each of us. I don't know whether that heavenly gate is pearly or not, but I do know, as do all students of the Book of Mormon, that the "keeper of the gate is the Holy One of Israel; and he employ[s] no servant there; . . . for the Lord God is his name."[29] Yes, each one of us will have a personal interview with Jesus Christ.

Each day on earth gives you time and opportunity to prepare for that interview. Know this: As you choose to live on the Lord's side, you are never alone. God has given you access to His help while you move along mortality's perilous pathway. As you diligently, earnestly pour your heart out to Him in daily prayer, He will send His angels to help you.[30] He has given you the Holy Ghost to be by your side as you live worthily. He has given you scriptures so you can fully feast upon the words of Jesus Christ.[31] He has given you words to heed from living prophets.

He has given you opportunity to receive a patriarchal blessing. It will provide insight about your connection to Abraham, Isaac, Jacob, and the covenant made with them for their posterity. Your patriarchal blessing also provides insight about your potential in life here and hereafter. Each of these and other divine aids will help you to choose well, so that you may look forward to meeting with your Savior face-to-face.

My last question: In whom will you put your trust?

You know that God is your Father. He loves you. He wants you to be happy. Put your trust in Him.[32] Maintain your focus on His holy temple. Be worthy to receive your endowment and sealing ordinances. Remain faithful to those covenants and return frequently to the temple. Remember, your loftiest goal is to gain the greatest of all the blessings of God, that of eternal life. Ordinances of the temple are essential to that blessing.[33]

I invite you to study prayerfully the scriptural statement

of your identity, purpose, and blessing as recorded in section 86 of the Doctrine and Covenants. It is all about you!

"Thus saith the Lord unto you, with whom the priesthood hath continued through the lineage of your fathers—

"For ye are lawful heirs, according to the flesh, and have been hid from the world with Christ in God—

"Therefore *your* life and the priesthood have remained, and must needs remain through *you* and your lineage until the restoration of all things spoken by the mouths of all the holy prophets since the world began.

"Therefore, blessed are *ye* if ye continue in my goodness, a light unto the Gentiles, and through this priesthood, a savior unto my people Israel."[34]

Yes, you are truly of the noble birthright, created in God's image. You are His lawful heir, here to be tried and tested. You may choose to be a light to the world, to help save God's children, to have joy, and ultimately to earn the blessing of eternal life.

The fulness of the earth is promised to those who

KEEP THE

Sabbath Day

HOLY.

CHAPTER 12

WE CAN MAKE THE SABBATH A DELIGHT

I am intrigued by the words of Isaiah, who called the Sabbath "a delight."[1] Yet I wonder, is the Sabbath really a delight for you and for me?

I first found delight in the Sabbath many years ago when, as a busy surgeon, I knew that the Sabbath became a day for personal healing. By the end of each week, my hands were sore from repeatedly scrubbing them with soap, water, and a bristle brush. I also needed a breather from the burden of a demanding profession. Sunday provided much-needed relief.

What did the Savior mean when He said that "the sabbath was made for man, and not man for the sabbath"?[2] I believe He wanted us to understand that the Sabbath was His gift to us, granting real respite from the rigors of daily life and an opportunity for spiritual and physical renewal. God gave us this special day, not for amusement or daily labor but for a rest from duty, with physical and spiritual relief.

In Hebrew, the word *Sabbath* means "rest." The purpose of the Sabbath dates back to the Creation of the world, when after six days of labor the Lord rested from the work of creation.[3] When He later revealed the Ten Commandments to Moses, God commanded that we "remember the sabbath day, to keep it holy."[4] Later, the Sabbath was observed as a reminder of the deliverance of Israel from their bondage in Egypt.[5] Perhaps most important, the Sabbath was given as a perpetual covenant, a constant reminder that the Lord may sanctify His people.[6]

In addition, we now partake of the sacrament on the Sabbath day in remembrance of the Atonement of Jesus Christ.[7] Again, we covenant that we are willing to take upon us His holy name.[8]

The Savior identified Himself as Lord of the Sabbath.[9] It is His day! Repeatedly, He has asked us to *keep* the Sabbath[10] or to *hallow* the Sabbath day.[11] We are under covenant to do so.

How do we *hallow* the Sabbath day? In my much younger years, I studied the work of others who had compiled lists of things to do and things *not* to do on the Sabbath. It wasn't until later that I learned from the scriptures that my conduct and my attitude on the Sabbath constituted a *sign* between me and my Heavenly Father.[12] With that understanding, I no longer needed lists of dos and don'ts. When I had to make a decision whether or not an activity was appropriate for the Sabbath, I simply asked myself, "What *sign* do I want to give to God?" That question made my choices about the Sabbath day crystal clear.

Though the doctrine pertaining to the Sabbath day is of ancient origin, it has been renewed in these latter days as part of a new covenant with a promise. Listen to the power of this divine decree:

"That thou mayest more fully keep thyself unspotted from the world, thou shalt go to the house of prayer and offer up thy sacraments upon my holy day;

"For verily this is a day appointed unto you to rest from your labors, and to pay thy devotions unto the Most High. . . .

"And on this day . . . let thy food be prepared with singleness of heart that thy fasting may be perfect, . . . that thy joy may be full. . . .

"And inasmuch as ye do these things with thanksgiving, with cheerful hearts and countenances, . . . the fulness of the earth is yours."[13]

Imagine the scope of that statement! The fulness of the earth is promised to those who keep the Sabbath day holy.[14] No wonder Isaiah called the Sabbath "a delight."

How can you ensure that your behavior on the Sabbath

will lead to joy and rejoicing? In addition to your going to church, partaking of the sacrament, and being diligent in your specific call to serve, what other activities would help to make the Sabbath a delight for you? What sign will you give to the Lord to show your love for Him?

The Sabbath provides a wonderful opportunity to strengthen family ties. After all, God wants each of us, as His children, to return to Him as endowed Saints, sealed in the temple as families, to our ancestors, and to our posterity.[15]

Parents have such wonderful resources available to help them make family time more meaningful, on the Sabbath and other days as well. They have LDS.org, Mormon.org, the Bible videos, the Mormon Channel, the Media Library, the *Friend,* the *New Era,* the *Ensign,* the *Liahona,* and more—much more. These resources are so very helpful to parents in discharging their sacred duty to teach their children. No other work transcends that of righteous, intentional parenting!

As you teach the gospel, you will learn more. This is the Lord's way of helping you to comprehend His gospel. He said:

"I give unto you a commandment that you shall teach one another the doctrine of the kingdom.

"Teach ye diligently . . . , that you may be instructed

more perfectly . . . in doctrine, in the law of the gospel, in all things that pertain unto the kingdom of God."[16]

Such study of the gospel makes the Sabbath a delight. This promise pertains regardless of family size, composition, or location.

In addition to time with family, you can experience true delight on the Sabbath from family history work. Searching for and finding family members who have preceded you on earth—those who did not have an opportunity to accept the gospel while here—can bring immense joy.

I have seen this firsthand. Several years ago, my dear wife Wendy determined to learn how to do family history research. Her progress at first was slow, but little by little she learned how easy it is to do this sacred work. And I have never seen her happier. You too need not travel to other countries or even to a family history center. At home, with the aid of a computer or mobile device, you can identify souls who are yearning for their ordinances. Make the Sabbath a delight by finding your ancestors and liberating them from spirit prison![17]

Make the Sabbath a delight by rendering service to others, especially those who are not feeling well or those who are lonely or in need.[18] Lifting their spirits will lift yours as well.

When Isaiah described the Sabbath as "a delight," he also taught us how to make it delightful. He said:

"If thou turn away . . . from doing thy pleasure on my holy day; and call the sabbath a delight, . . . and shalt honour [the Lord], not doing thine own ways, nor finding thine own pleasure, nor speaking thine own words:

"Then shalt thou delight thyself *in the Lord.*"[19]

Not pursuing your "own pleasure" on the Sabbath requires self-discipline. You may have to deny yourself of something you might like. If you choose to delight yourself *in the Lord,* you will not permit yourself to treat it as any other day. Routine and recreational activities can be done some other time.

Think of this: In paying tithing, we return one-tenth of our increase to the Lord. In keeping the Sabbath holy, we reserve one day in seven as His. So it is our privilege to consecrate both money and time to Him who lends us life each day.[20]

We know that wherever we live we are to be examples of the believers among our families, neighbors, and friends.[21] True believers keep the Sabbath day holy.

Faith in God engenders a love for the Sabbath; faith in the Sabbath engenders a love for God. A sacred Sabbath truly is a delight.

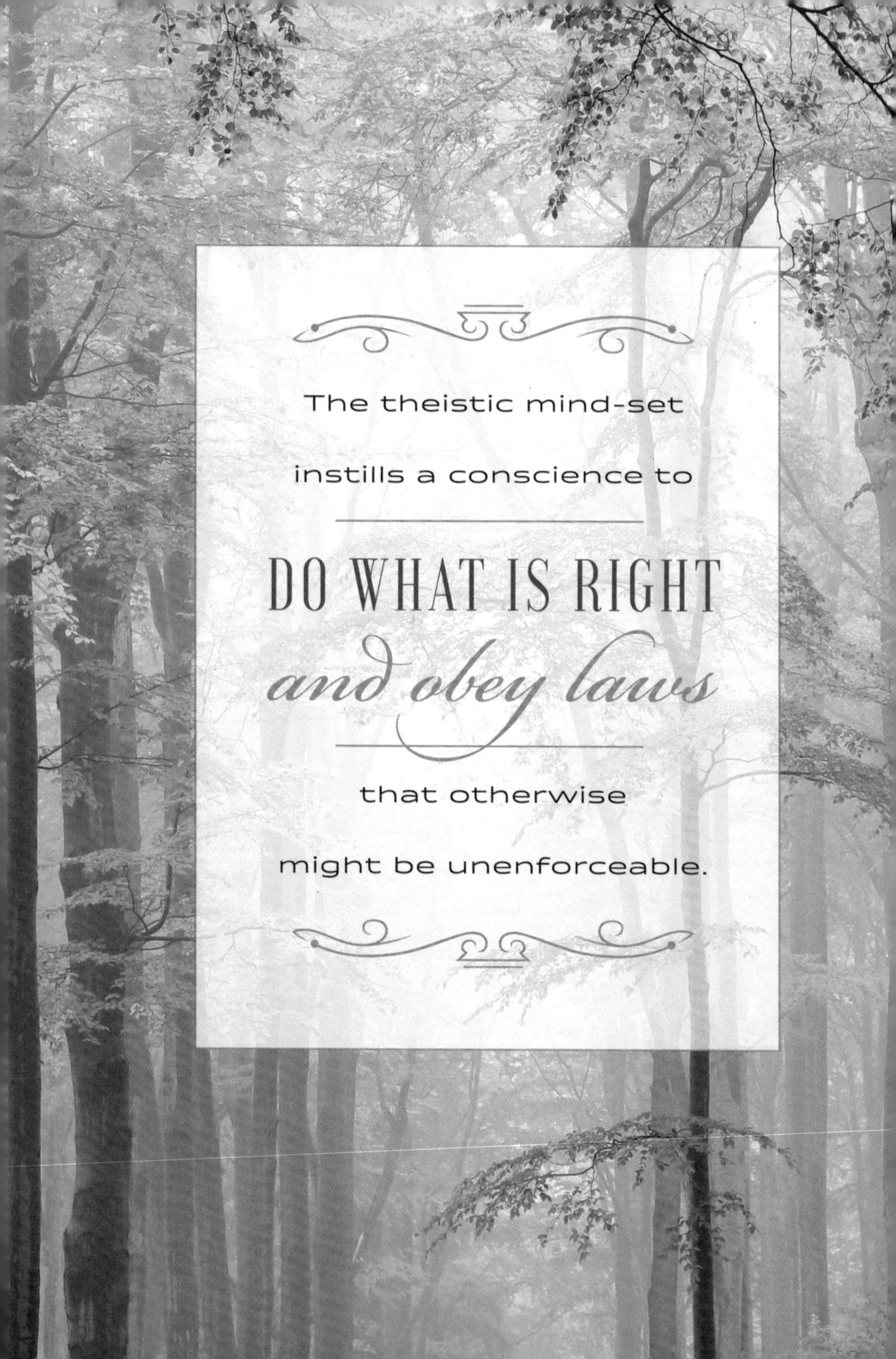
The theistic mind-set
instills a conscience to
DO WHAT IS RIGHT
and obey laws
that otherwise
might be unenforceable.

CONCLUSION

THE WORLD NEEDS OUR CONTRIBUTION

I love the poetic words and message of a favorite hymn:

Behold! A royal army,
With banner, sword, and shield,
Is marching forth to conquer
On life's great battlefield.
Its ranks are filled with soldiers,
United, bold, and strong,
Who follow their Commander
And sing their joyful song:
Victory, victory,
Thru him that redeemed us!
Victory, victory,
Thru Jesus Christ, our Lord![1]

Yes, the Lord is our commander; we are His soldiers in a

mighty war. The conflict in which we are engaged is between the forces of God and the forces of the adversary.[2] This conflict began before the world was created. It began with the war in heaven. On God's side was Jesus Christ, foreordained to be the Savior of the world.[3]

This conflict continues here on earth. We as servants of the Lord are advocates of joy. We know that "men are, that they might have joy."[4] In contrast, the way of the adversary always leads to misery, despair, and destruction.

Thus, opposing forces are competing for our allegiance: right versus wrong, good versus evil.[5] These forces are, in fact, conflicting religious systems of belief. They are theistic (godly) forces and atheistic (ungodly or satanic) forces. These were cited by Elder Clayton Christensen in an editorial calling for theistic balance on the U.S. Supreme Court.[6] I would like to extend his views and apply them to the challenges we so often face.

Theistic forces, be they Islamic, Jewish, Catholic, Protestant, or Mormon, teach that there is an absolute right and wrong. Theistic forces have an ethic that reveres the righteous judgments of a loving God and obeys civil and divine law voluntarily. The theistic mind-set instills a conscience to do what is right and obey laws that otherwise might be unenforceable.

With such a commitment, you obey a red stop light, even

if no other traffic is in sight. As a God-fearing person, you know that even if the police didn't catch you if you were to steal, murder, or commit adultery, these acts are wrong, and God will ultimately hold you accountable. You know, just as your ancestors knew, that the consequences for not playing by the rules are not only temporal, but also eternal. These theistic forces were a part of the shaping of America. From the Book of Mormon, we have learned that this is a "land of promise, . . . choice above all other lands, which the Lord God had preserved for a *righteous* people."[7]

Granted, there are people in America who are not religious who also obey unenforceable laws. Why? Because they live in a theistic culture. Although they may try to invent some sort of happiness for themselves outside God and without acknowledging Him as the ultimate source of true joy, they still draw power from the theism of their ancestors. Their culture is good because theistic forces have endowed them with a rich culture of righteousness. Unfortunately, good culture alone is not strong enough to cause good culture to endure in perpetuity. Additional strength is needed from the power of theistic conviction.

For this reason, a policy to separate church and state completely could become completely counterproductive. The effect of erasing a theistic culture would allow atheistic forces to flourish unopposed in the public square. If that happens, the theistic and noble concept of "freedom of religion" could be twisted and turned to become an atheistic "freedom from religion." Such an unbalanced policy could sweep out the theistic forces that have been responsible for our society's success and leave the field wide open to atheistic ideology, secularism, and huge losses for each of us.

This scenario was foreseen by our Master, who taught that such people "seek not the Lord to establish his righteousness, but every man walketh in his own way, and after the image of his own god, whose image is in the likeness of the world."[8]

Without an acknowledgment of God and God's law in one's life, momentary pleasures will be continually contaminated by gnawing guilt. Momentary pleasures would become meaningless as each raw experience would be stripped of deep meaning and sweet memory. Each day's work would become sheer drudgery, beauties of nature would become boring, and children would be deemed nuisances to be endured. Without God's moral underpinnings, political behavior would be skewed toward short-term expediency, lurching nervously from crisis to crisis.

One of society's skirmishes today is over the very definition of marriage. In heated debate is the question of whether two people of the same gender can be married. But that question is only the tip of the iceberg. Below this tip is the weightier matter of free exercise of religion. Contention is raging over two main issues:

1. Can marriage survive as the bedrock of our cultural heritage?
2. Can our precious freedom of religion be preserved?

At stake is our ability to transmit to the next generation the life-giving and inseparable culture of marriage and the free exercise of religion. The theistic marriage of a man and a woman allows for the most holy of all human relationships—the begetting of children—through the sacred marital embrace, enabled by the divine design of Almighty God.

Atheistic counterfeits were foreseen in our day by the Apostle Paul, written in an epistle to Timothy. It is a warning to all of us:

"In the last days perilous times shall come.

"For men shall be lovers of their own selves, covetous, boasters, proud, blasphemers, disobedient to parents, unthankful, unholy,

"Without natural affection, trucebreakers, false accusers, incontinent, fierce, despisers of those that are good,

"Traitors, heady, highminded, lovers of pleasures more than lovers of God;

"Having a form of godliness, but denying the power thereof: from such turn away."[9]

Paul's prophetic description of our day was followed by his prescription for protection. This was his reassuring conclusion: "That from a child thou hast known the holy scriptures, which are able to make thee wise unto salvation through faith which is in Christ Jesus."[10]

As you hold fast to the iron rod of the gospel, you will gain strength to fulfill your divine destiny. Be strong, stalwart soldiers in the army of God, protected by His doctrinal armor, helmet of salvation, and shield of faith.[11]

Your challenges in life are best understood in the light of divine perspective. Trials and tests are necessary for your education and refinement. This doctrine is stated in the 101st section of the Doctrine and Covenants. Speaking of those who will be gathered into the fold of Christ, Jesus said, "Yet I will own them, and they shall be mine in that day when I shall come to make up my jewels.

"Therefore, they must needs be chastened and tried, even as Abraham, who was commanded to offer up his only son.

"For all those who will not endure chastening, but deny me, cannot be sanctified."[12]

Each Church leader you sustain as a prophet, seer, and revelator has endured or will endure such an Abrahamic test. At some time you, too, will also be tried and tested, even more than you already have been. Develop now a faith sufficient to sustain you through that difficult time.

As you feast upon the words of Jesus Christ, you will understand His doctrine and be able to apply His teachings in your lives. If you will live as He would have you live, through your example of righteousness, you will become worthy of emulation as a member of the Church that bears His holy name.

So I say to you, foster your faith. Fix your focus with an eye single to the glory of God. "Be strong and courageous,"[13] and you will be given power and protection from on high. The Lord has declared His sustaining help: "Fear thou not; for I am with thee: be not dismayed; for I am thy God: I will strengthen thee; yea, I will help thee; yea, I will uphold thee with the right hand of my righteousness."[14]

The Lord has more in mind for you than you have in mind for yourself! You have been reserved and preserved for this time and place. You can do hard things. At the same time, as you love Him and keep His commandments, great rewards—even unimaginable achievements—may be yours. Indeed, "eye hath not seen, nor ear heard, neither have entered into the heart of man, the things which God hath prepared for them that love him."[15]

The Lord needs you to change the world. As you accept and follow His will for you, you will find yourself accomplishing the impossible!

NOTES

Introduction: Accomplishing the Impossible

1. See Doctrine and Covenants 13; 110; Joseph Smith—History 1:30–47, 49.
2. See 1 Samuel 17:49–50.
3. Judges 7:2–7.
4. Judges 7:12 states, "The Midianites and the Amalekites and all the children of the east lay along in the valley like grasshoppers for multitude; and their camels were without number, as the sand by the sea side for multitude."

   Gideon pursued the Midianites to Karkor, where they numbered "about fifteen thousand men, all that were left of all the hosts of the children of the east: for there fell an hundred and twenty thousand men that drew sword" (Judges 8:10). This would seem to imply that this was the number that Gideon pursued. This idea is confirmed in *Harper's Bible Dictionary* (1985), 347.
5. See Exodus 3:8–12.
6. See Exodus 14:21–22.
7. See Joshua 3:13–17.
8. Acts 3:21.
9. See Russell M. Nelson, "'With God Nothing Shall Be Impossible,'" *Ensign*, May 1988, 33.
10. See James Avery Joyce, sel., *World Population Basic Documents,* 4 vols. (1976), 4:2214.
11. Matthew 19:26; see also Matthew 17:20; Mark 10:27; Luke 1:37; 18:27.

12. 1 Corinthians 1:27.
13. 2 Nephi 27:21.
14. Luke 1:37.
15. See Doctrine and Covenants 1:20.

Chapter 1: He Sends Angels

1. See Matthew 16:19; 17:1–3.
2. See Doctrine and Covenants 27:12.
3. See Doctrine and Covenants 13:1; 27:7.
4. See Doctrine and Covenants 27:5.
5. Revelation 14:6.
6. The two gammas together (Γ Γ) are pronounced as "ng."
7. Luke 2:10–11.
8. Joseph Smith—History 1:17; italics in original.
9. Doctrine and Covenants 76:20.
10. Doctrine and Covenants 76:20–23.
11. Doctrine and Covenants 137:3.
12. Doctrine and Covenants 137:9.
13. Doctrine and Covenants 137:10.
14. Doctrine and Covenants 110:2–4.
15. Doctrine and Covenants 110:11.
16. Doctrine and Covenants 110:12.
17. See Genesis 17:1–10; 22:15–18; Galatians 3:26–29; Abraham 2:9–11.
18. See Genesis 26:1–5, 24.
19. See Genesis 28:1–4, 10–14; 35:9–13; 48:3–4.
20. Doctrine and Covenants 110:13–15.
21. See Doctrine and Covenants 2:1–3.
22. See Malachi 4:5–6.
23. Bible Dictionary, s.v. "Malachi," 728.
24. See Daniel 10:13, 21; 12:1; Jude 1:9; Revelation 12:7; Bible Dictionary, s.v. "Michael," 732.
25. See Doctrine and Covenants 27:11; 107:53–56; 128:21.
26. See Daniel 8:16; 9:21.
27. See Luke 1:11–19.
28. See Luke 1:26–38.
29. See Joseph Smith, *History of the Church of Jesus Christ of Latter-day Saints*, 7 vols. (1932–51), 3:386.
30. Doctrine and Covenants 84:28.
31. See Matthew 14:3–10; Mark 6:27.
32. 3 Nephi 7:15–16, 18.
33. Moroni 7:36–37.

34. Doctrine and Covenants 128:21.
35. See 3 Nephi 28:6–7; Doctrine and Covenants 7:1–8.
36. See 3 Nephi 28:1–6.
37. 3 Nephi 28:30.
38. Doctrine and Covenants 84:88.
39. This incident occurred on May 29, 2009.

Chapter 2: He Blesses Us with Peace and Love

1. John 3:16.
2. See Isaiah 9:6; 2 Nephi 19:6.
3. *Messiah* in Hebrew and *Christ* in Greek both mean "anointed."
4. See Moses 1:32–33.
5. See 1 John 2:1; Doctrine and Covenants 29:5; 110:4.
6. See Isaiah 7:14; 2 Nephi 17:14; see also Matthew 1:23.
7. See Abraham 1:16; 2:8; Exodus 3:11–14; 6:3.
8. See 3 Nephi 27:13–14.
9. See Moses 1:39.
10. See 3 Nephi 27:21.
11. See 2 Nephi 9:41.
12. Matthew 19:14.
13. See Luke 2:14.
14. 3 Nephi 17:7.
15. 3 Nephi 17:8; see also Matthew 13:15; 3 Nephi 18:32; Doctrine and Covenants 112:13.
16. 2 Timothy 2:22.
17. Jeremiah 8:22.
18. John Newton, *Olney Hymns* (1779); see also John 9:25.
19. Luke 15:7; see also v. 10.
20. Matthew 11:28–30.
21. Matthew 5:4; see also 3 Nephi 12:4.
22. Doctrine and Covenants 42:46.
23. John 14:27.
24. John 11:25–26.
25. John 14:15.
26. Luke 18:22.
27. 1 John 4:7–8.
28. Mosiah 5:7.
29. 3 Nephi 27:20.
30. 3 Nephi 27:27.
31. See 1 Nephi 17:35–44; Mosiah 7:20; Alma 9:9–11; 3 Nephi 5:20–22.

32. See Book of Mormon title page; 1 Nephi 13:35–41; 2 Nephi 33:4; Mosiah 1:2–7; Mormon 8:13–16.
33. John 10:16; see also 3 Nephi 15:11–24.
34. 3 Nephi 11:11.
35. 3 Nephi 11:14.
36. See 3 Nephi 11–14; 18–20.
37. 3 Nephi 17:21–24.
38. See "We'll Sing All Hail to Jesus' Name," *Hymns* (1985), no. 182.
39. Isaiah 40:5.
40. See Revelation 19:16.
41. See Doctrine and Covenants 14:7.

Chapter 3: He Gives Us Physical and Spiritual Gifts

1. John 6:35, 48; see also verse 51.
2. Alma 26:8; see also Alma 7:23.
3. See Acts 17:27–29.
4. See Doctrine and Covenants 130:22.
5. See Moses 6:51; see also Jeremiah 1:4–5; Romans 8:16; Hebrews 12:9.
6. See Genesis 2:7; 1 Corinthians 15:44; Moses 3:7.
7. See 1 Nephi 17:36.
8. Moses 1:39.
9. John 3:16.
10. John 3:17.
11. His purposes are succinctly summarized in 3 Nephi 27:13–22.
12. See Alma 11:40.
13. See 2 Nephi 9:6–7, 20–22.
14. John 11:25–26.
15. See 1 Nephi 17:40; 1 John 4:10.
16. 2 Peter 1:4.
17. The heart pumps about 2,000 gallons (7,570 liters) per day.
18. Doctrine and Covenants 88:47.
19. See Doctrine and Covenants 130:21. Indeed that divine law is incontrovertible.
20. Alma 42:8.
21. The Psalmist expressed the viewpoint of Deity: "Precious in the sight of the Lord is the death of his saints" (Psalm 116:15); see also Ecclesiastes 12:7.
22. Alma 11:43; see also Alma 40:23; Doctrine and Covenants 138:17.
23. See Doctrine and Covenants 93:38.
24. See Alma 40:11; Abraham 3:18.

25. The spirit is in the likeness of the person (see Doctrine and Covenants 77:2).
26. See 3 Nephi 14:9–11.
27. The spirit, not the body, is the active, responsible component of the soul. Without the spirit, the body is dead (see James 2:26). It is the spirit, therefore, that chooses good or evil and will be held accountable for both the positive and negative attributes it possesses at the Final Judgment (see Alma 41:3–7).
28. Spiritual attributes also include "faith, virtue, knowledge, temperance, patience, brotherly kindness, godliness, charity, humility, [and] diligence" (Doctrine and Covenants 4:6).
29. See 2 Nephi 2:11–16, 21–26; Moroni 10:32–33.
30. This is the doctrine of Christ (see 2 Nephi 31:11–21).
31. Mosiah 15:28; see also 1 Nephi 19:17; 2 Nephi 26:13; Mosiah 3:20; 15:28; 16:1; Alma 37:4; Doctrine and Covenants 1:18–23; 77:11; 133:37.
32. Mosiah 4:9–10.
33. "Eternal life . . . is the greatest of all the gifts of God" (Doctrine and Covenants 14:7).

Chapter 4: He Teaches Us to Pray

1. The January 1976 issue of the *Ensign* was published as a special issue on prayer. The sincere student of prayer will gain much from a study of those articles.
2. Matthew 6:9–13.
3. See Matthew 6:9–13; Luke 11:2–4; 3 Nephi 13:9–13.
4. See Joseph Smith Translation, Matthew 6:9–15.
5. Joseph Smith Translation, Matthew 6:13.
6. Joseph Smith Translation, Matthew 6:14.
7. Doctrine and Covenants 82:1.
8. See Matthew 18:23–35; Doctrine and Covenants 64:10.
9. Matthew 26:41.
10. John 6:35; see also John 6:48, 51.
11. See Moroni 4:3; 5:2; Doctrine and Covenants 20:77, 79.
12. In the Hebrew and Greek languages, *amen* means "truly," "surely," "verily," or "so be it."
13. See Revelation 1:18; 22:20–21. It is also used in confirming agreements (see 1 Kings 1:36).
14. See 1 Corinthians 14:16.
15. See Psalm 106:48; Revelation 5:13–14; 19:4; Doctrine and Covenants 88:135.
16. Matthew 6:7; 3 Nephi 13:7.

17. Matthew 6:9; 3 Nephi 13:9.
18. John 17:1, 4, 8–9.
19. See 1 Timothy 2:5; 1 John 2:1; Doctrine and Covenants 29:5; 45:3; 110:4.
20. See Doctrine and Covenants 14:7.
21. 3 Nephi 17:17.
22. 3 Nephi 17:20.
23. 3 Nephi 19:23.
24. See Matthew 5:44; Alma 34:27; 3 Nephi 18:21.
25. James 5:16.
26. 3 Nephi 18:19.
27. 3 Nephi 18:21.
28. See 2 Nephi 32:9; 33:12; 3 Nephi 18:23, 30; 19:6–7; 20:31; 28:30.
29. 3 Nephi 19:20–22.
30. See John 10:27–28 (compare Doctrine and Covenants 84:43–47); 2 Nephi 31:17–20; Alma 5:38. And we may invite the companionship of the Spirit, who will intercede and help us know what to pray about (see Romans 8:26).
31. Doctrine and Covenants 25:12.
32. See Acts 14:23; 1 Corinthians 7:5; Omni 1:26; Alma 5:46; 6:6; 17:3, 9; 28:6; 45:1; 3 Nephi 27:1; 4 Nephi 1:12; Moroni 6:5.
33. Doctrine and Covenants 88:76.
34. Joseph F. Smith, in Conference Report, October 1912, 133–34.
35. Joseph Smith Translation, Psalm 17:1.
36. See Bruce R. McConkie, "Why the Lord Ordained Prayer," *Ensign,* January 1976, 12; L. Tom Perry, "Our Father Which Art in Heaven," *Ensign,* November 1983, 13; and Dallin H. Oaks, "The Language of Prayer," *Ensign*, May 1993, 15–18. Details of that language are explained by Don E. Norton Jr., "The Language of Formal Prayer," *Ensign,* January 1976, 44–47.
37. Doctrine and Covenants 112:10; see also Psalm 24:3–4; Helaman 3:35.
38. Revelation 3:20.
39. See 3 Nephi 18:20; Doctrine and Covenants 88:64.
40. Alma 37:37; see also Philippians 4:6; Alma 34:18–27; Doctrine and Covenants 10:5; 93:49.
41. 3 Nephi 20:1.
42. See McConkie, "Why the Lord Ordained Prayer," 11.
43. Thomas S. Monson, "A Royal Priesthood," *Ensign*, November 2007, 61.
44. See Matthew 26:42; Jacob 7:14; Ether 12:29; Doctrine and Covenants 109:44; Moses 4:2.
45. See 3 Nephi 27:13–15, 21–22.
46. Mosiah 15:7.

47. Matthew 26:39; see also Moses 4:2, which indicates the humble attitude of our Savior from the beginning.
48. Doctrine and Covenants 65:5.

Chapter 5: He Offers Covenants to Strengthen Us

1. That stake was created Sunday, June 5, 2011.
2. Vyacheslav Efimov was president of the Russia Yekaterinburg Mission from 1995 to 1998. He died February 25, 2000.
3. See Doctrine and Covenants 138:57.
4. Doctrine and Covenants 130:21.
5. For example, after the great Flood, He stated that "the bow shall be seen in the cloud: and I will remember my covenant, which I have made between me and you. . . . And the waters shall no more become a flood to destroy all flesh" (Genesis 9:14–15, footnote 15b; from Joseph Smith Translation, Genesis 9:20).
6. See Doctrine and Covenants 66:2; 133:57.
7. See John 3:16.
8. See Abraham 3:25.
9. Acts 3:25.
10. See 3 Nephi 20:26.
11. 3 Nephi 20:25.
12. 3 Nephi 20:26.
13. Deuteronomy 7:9; 1 Chronicles 16:15; Psalm 105:8.
14. 1 Nephi 15:18; emphasis added.
15. Doctrine and Covenants 132:30–31. The Lord also told the Prophet Joseph Smith: "As I said unto Abraham concerning the kindreds of the earth, even so I say unto my servant Joseph: In thee and in thy seed shall the kindred of the earth be blessed" (Doctrine and Covenants 124:58).
16. See Doctrine and Covenants 14:7.
17. See Acts 10:34–35.
18. See Exodus 19:5.
19. Scripture declares that "I, the Lord, am bound when ye do what I say; but when ye do not what I say, ye have no promise" (Doctrine and Covenants 82:10).
20. On September 21, 1823, this covenantal concept was first revealed to the Prophet Joseph Smith. Then the angel Moroni declared that Elijah the prophet would come as a messenger from heaven to plant in the hearts of the children a knowledge of promises once made to the fathers of the house of Israel (see Doctrine and Covenants 2:1–3).
21. See Doctrine and Covenants 84:33–34, 39–40.
22. Doctrine and Covenants 84:33.

23. See Doctrine and Covenants 84:35, 37.
24. See Doctrine and Covenants 84:38.
25. See Alma 13:1–9.
26. See 3 Nephi 29.
27. 3 Nephi 29:1, 3.
28. Title page of the Book of Mormon: Another Testament of Jesus Christ.
29. *Teachings of Presidents of the Church: Brigham Young* (1997), 62.
30. Bible Dictionary, s.v. "Temple."
31. See Doctrine and Covenants 124:33, 41; 128:5.
32. See Moses 5:5. The Old Testament has many references to temple activity and clothing (for example, see these chapters: Exodus 28, 29; Leviticus 8).
33. See Exodus 38:21.
34. John 2:16.
35. Matthew 21:13; Mark 11:17.
36. Matthew 23:38; Luke 13:35.
37. There, some six thousand ordinances were performed before the temple had to be abandoned. Rebuilt and rededicated in the year 2002, it now stands in full splendor and majesty.
38. See Susa Young Gates and Leah D. Widtsoe, *The Life Story of Brigham Young* (1930), 104–5.
39. *The Discourses of Wilford Woodruff,* sel. G. Homer Durham (1946), 154.
40. *Discourses of Brigham Young,* sel. John A. Widtsoe (1954), 403, 404.
41. "'Exceeding Great and Precious Promises,'" *Ensign,* November 1994, 8.
42. See Doctrine and Covenants 2:3; 138:48; Joseph Smith—History 1:39.
43. This concept pertains to us: "Many generations after the Messiah shall be manifested in body unto the children of men, then shall the fulness of the gospel of the Messiah come unto the Gentiles, and from the Gentiles unto the remnant of our seed—

    "And at that day shall the remnant of our seed know that they are of the house of Israel, and that they are the covenant people of the Lord; and then shall they know and come to the knowledge of their forefathers, and also to the knowledge of the gospel of their Redeemer, which was ministered unto their fathers by him; wherefore, they shall come to the knowledge of their Redeemer and the very points of his doctrine, that they may know how to come unto him and be saved" (1 Nephi 15:13–14).
44. See Isaiah 55:3; Jeremiah 31:33; Romans 2:15; 2 Corinthians 3:2–3; Hebrews 10:16.
45. See Psalms 95:7, 100:3; Jeremiah 24:7; 31:33; 32:38; Ezekiel 11:20; 37:23, 27; Zechariah 8:8; 2 Corinthians 6:16; Hebrews 8:10.
46. Mosiah 2:41.

Chapter 6: We Can Receive Revelation

1. Matthew 7:7; Luke 11:9; emphasis added; see also 3 Nephi 14:7; Joseph Smith Translation, Matthew 7:12.
2. Moroni 10:4.
3. Doctrine and Covenants 9:8.
4. 1 Corinthians 2:14.
5. See Mosiah 5:2; Alma 5:12–14.
6. Mosiah 3:19.
7. *Discern* comes from the Latin *discernere,* meaning "to separate [or] distinguish between." The Latin prefix *dis* means "apart," and the suffix *cernere* means "to sift." See *Merriam-Webster's Collegiate Dictionary*, 11th ed. (2003), "discern."
8. See Doctrine and Covenants 46:23, 26–27.
9. After the death of President Brigham Young in 1877, the affairs of the Church were directed by the Quorum of the Twelve Apostles. The apostolic interregnum continued until 1880, when the First Presidency was reorganized. John Taylor was President of the Quorum of the Twelve when this counsel was given on February 23, 1878.
10. In James R. Clark, comp., *Messages of the First Presidency of The Church of Jesus Christ of Latter-day Saints,* 6 vols. (1965–75), 2:307.
11. Doctrine and Covenants 4:5–6; see also verse 7.
12. Doctrine and Covenants 76:5–7.
13. 2 Nephi 28:30.
14. Doctrine and Covenants 110:1.
15. Doctrine and Covenants 138:11. Then followed the revelation about the preaching of the gospel to those who had died without an opportunity to hear the gospel in mortality (see verses 29–37).
16. See Doctrine and Covenants 1:30.

Chapter 7: We Can Overcome Temptation

1. Thomas S. Monson, "Decisions Determine Destiny" (Church Educational System fireside, November 6, 2005), 3; speeches.byu.edu.
2. The concept of eternal progression was captured well by W. W. Phelps in his text to the hymn "If You Could Hie to Kolob" (*Hymns* [1985], no. 284). Verse 4 reads: "There is no end to virtue; / There is no end to might; / There is no end to wisdom; / There is no end to light. / There is no end to union; / There is no end to youth; / There is no end to priesthood; / There is no end to truth." Verse 5 concludes: "There is no end to glory; / There is no end to love; / There is no end to being; / There is no death above."
3. Genesis 1:27; see also Colossians 3:10; Alma 18:34; Ether 3:15; Moses 6:9.

4. See "I Am a Child of God," *Hymns,* no. 301.
5. See Matthew 10:37.
6. See Mark 12:30–31.
7. See Doctrine and Covenants 88:15.
8. 1 Corinthians 3:16; see also 6:19.
9. Abraham 3:23.
10. See Jeremiah 1:5.
11. See Alma 13:2–3.
12. See Doctrine and Covenants 138:55–56.
13. See Alma 13:2–3; Doctrine and Covenants 138:38–57.
14. Attributes of "faith, virtue, knowledge, temperance, patience, brotherly kindness, godliness, charity, humility, [and] diligence" (Doctrine and Covenants 4:6) are among the spiritual gifts we can develop and be given. Gratitude is another spiritual attribute that can be developed. Gratitude shapes mood and productivity. And when you have "spiritually been born of God," you may gratefully receive His image in your countenance (see Alma 5:14).
15. See 1 Corinthians 12; 14:1–12; Moroni 10:8–19; Doctrine and Covenants 46:10–29.
16. Some are tempted to eat too much. "Obesity has reached epidemic proportions globally, with at least 2.8 million people dying each year as a result of being overweight" ("10 Facts on Obesity," World Health Organization, March 2013, www.who.int/features/factfiles/obesity/en). Others are tempted to eat too little. Anorexia and bulimia devastate many lives, marriages, and families. And some are tempted by sexual appetites forbidden by our Creator. Clarification is found in *Handbook 2: Administering the Church,* which states: "The Lord's law of chastity is abstinence from sexual relations outside of lawful marriage and fidelity within marriage. . . . Adultery, fornication, homosexual or lesbian relations, and every other unholy, unnatural, or impure practice are sinful." Still quoting from the handbook: "Homosexual behavior violates the commandments of God, is contrary to the purposes of human sexuality, and deprives people of the blessings that can be found in family life and in the saving ordinances of the gospel. . . . While opposing homosexual behavior, the Church reaches out with understanding and respect to individuals who are attracted to those of the same gender" ([2010], 21.4.5; 21.4.6).
17. See 1 Corinthians 6:9–20; James 1:25–27; Doctrine and Covenants 130:20–21. And we should always remember that "men are, that they might have joy" (2 Nephi 2:25).
18. Mortality is a period of testing, as explained in scripture: "We will prove

them herewith, to see if they will do all things whatsoever the Lord their God shall command them" (Abraham 3:25).

19. See Mosiah 4:10; Alma 39:9; Helaman 15:7.
20. Through the Atonement of Jesus Christ and by obedience to the principles of the gospel, all mankind may be saved (see Doctrine and Covenants 138:4; Articles of Faith 1:3).
21. See Ether 12:33–34; Moroni 8:17.
22. See Mosiah 5:2; Alma 5:12–14.
23. See Romans 8:13–17; Galatians 5:13–25; Doctrine and Covenants 88:86.
24. 2 Nephi 2:27.
25. See Doctrine and Covenants 131:1–4.
26. "The Family: A Proclamation to the World," *Ensign,* November 2010, 129.
27. See Matthew 19:4–6; Mosiah 29:26–27; Helaman 5:2.
28. Each person is born with unique identity, chromosomes, and DNA (deoxyribonucleic acid). DNA is a molecule that encodes genetic instructions used in the development and function of living cells. Each person's DNA is created when the DNA from a father and a mother combine to create the DNA of a new body—a partnership between father, mother, and child.
29. See Genesis 2:24–25; 3:20–21; 4:1–2, 25.
30. Dr. Patrick F. Fagan wrote: "The indispensable building block upon which the fortunes of the economy depends [is] the married-parent household—especially the child-rich family that worships weekly. . . . Every marriage creates a new household, an independent economic unit that generates income, spends, saves, and invests" ("The Family GDP: How Marriage and Fertility Drive the Economy," *The Family in America,* vol. 24, no. 2 [Spring 2010], 136).
31. See Exodus 20:14; Leviticus 18:22; 20:13; Deuteronomy 5:18; Matthew 5:27–28; Mark 10:19; Luke 18:20; Romans 1:26–27; 13:9; Mosiah 13:22; 3 Nephi 12:27–28; Doctrine and Covenants 42:24; 59:6.
32. See Gordon B. Hinckley, "This Thing Was Not Done in a Corner," *Ensign,* November 1996, 49.
33. See Doctrine and Covenants 14:7.
34. See Moses 1:39.
35. See 2 Nephi 9:41, 46; Mosiah 16:10.
36. We will be judged according to our deeds and the desires of our hearts (see Doctrine and Covenants 137:9; see also Hebrews 4:12; Alma 18:32; Doctrine and Covenants 6:16; 88:109).

Chapter 8: We Can Act in Faith

1. When a baby is born, the umbilical cord is doubly ligated and severed between those two ligatures. A ligature is a tie—a secure tie. The word

religion comes from Latin roots, *re* meaning "again" or "back to," and likely *ligare*, meaning "to tie" or "to ligate." Thus, we understand that religion "ties believers to God."

2. Exodus 20:3. In addition, the Lord said, "Repent, and turn yourselves from your idols; and turn . . . from all your abominations" (Ezekiel 14:6).
3. Doctrine and Covenants 6:36.
4. See Spencer W. Kimball, *The Teachings of Spencer W. Kimball*, ed. Edward L. Kimball (1982), 391.
5. See Mosiah 2:41; Doctrine and Covenants 58:30–33; 82:10. This principle is true for everyone, for "God is no respecter of persons" (Acts 10:34); see also Moroni 8:12.
6. Doctrine and Covenants 132:22.
7. See Leviticus 15:13.
8. 2 Timothy 3:7.
9. 1 Nephi 19:23.
10. Isaiah 5:20.
11. Scripture teaches, "Come unto the Lord, the Holy One. Remember that his paths are righteous. Behold, the way for man is narrow, but it lieth in a straight course before him, and the keeper of the gate is the Holy One of Israel; and he employeth no servant there; and there is none other way save it be by the gate; for he cannot be deceived, for the Lord God is his name" (2 Nephi 9:41).
12. Thomas S. Monson, "Courage Counts," *Ensign*, November 1986, 40. On another occasion, President Monson gave this inspiring admonition: "To live greatly, we must develop the capacity to face trouble with courage, disappointment with cheerfulness, and triumph with humility. . . . We are sons and daughters of a living God in whose image we have been created. . . . We cannot sincerely hold this conviction without experiencing a profound new sense of strength and power, even the strength to live the commandments of God, the power to resist the temptations of Satan" (*Pathways to Perfection* [1973], 81–82).
13. "Deny yourself of all ungodliness" (Moroni 10:32). Do not fear man more than God (see Doctrine and Covenants 3:7; 59:5).

Chapter 9: We Can Share the Gospel

1. Matthew 28:19–20.
2. See Acts 9:3–18.
3. Acts 9:1.
4. 1 Timothy 4:12; emphasis added.
5. *Preach My Gospel: A Guide to Missionary Service* (2004), 1.
6. See Doctrine and Covenants 14:7.

7. Moses 1:39.
8. Luke 10:2.
9. See Thomas S. Monson, "Welcome to Conference," *Ensign*, November 2012, 4–5.
10. See Doctrine and Covenants 132:7, 19.
11. Doctrine and Covenants 88:73.
12. Joseph Smith—History 1:17; emphasis in original.
13. See John 17:3.
14. See Moses 1:39.
15. Alma 5:19.
16. See Matthew 5:16; Alma 7:24.
17. See Doctrine and Covenants 88:11.
18. 1 Peter 3:15.
19. See 2 Nephi 31:2, 21.
20. John 10:27.
21. John 1:39. For this pattern, see also Revelation 6:1, 3, 5, 7.
22. Title page of the Book of Mormon.
23. Introduction to the Book of Mormon.
24. See 3 Nephi 21:1–7. Note that these seven verses comprise one sentence.
25. Doctrine and Covenants 29:7.
26. Doctrine and Covenants 123:12.
27. Personal communication from mission president William G. Woods.
28. See Malachi 4:5; 3 Nephi 25:5; Doctrine and Covenants 2:1; 110:14–16; 128:17; 138:46; Joseph Smith—History 1:38.

Chapter 10: We Can Strengthen Our Families

1. Mark 10:6–8; emphasis added.
2. Doctrine and Covenants 2:3; see also Doctrine and Covenants 138:48; Joseph Smith—History 1:39.
3. Eternal life is "the greatest of all the gifts of God" (Doctrine and Covenants 14:7).
4. See Doctrine and Covenants 124:33.
5. Doctrine and Covenants 128:24.
6. See Isaiah 61:1; Luke 4:18; Doctrine and Covenants 138:18, 31, 42.
7. Doctrine and Covenants 64:10.
8. See Doctrine and Covenants 121:41–44.
9. See Moses 6:58–62.
10. Matthew 19:14; see also Mark 10:14; Luke 18:16.
11. See 2 Nephi 2:27.
12. Peter taught this concept when he expressed the hope that "ye might be

partakers of the divine nature, having escaped the corruption that is in the world" (2 Peter 1:4).

13. See Abraham 3:25.
14. See 2 Nephi 2:25.
15. See Doctrine and Covenants 89:19; Isaiah 45:3.
16. Doctrine and Covenants 84:88.
17. Doctrine and Covenants 122:7. Another example of change of perspective is recorded in Psalms: "Preserve my soul; . . . my God, save thy servant that trusteth in thee. Be merciful unto me, O Lord: for I cry unto thee daily. . . . I will praise thee, O Lord my God, with all my heart: and I will glorify thy name for evermore" (Psalm 86:2–3, 12).
18. Doctrine and Covenants 98:2–3.
19. Tithing is mentioned in eight books of the Old Testament: Genesis, Leviticus, Numbers, Deuteronomy, 2 Chronicles, Nehemiah, Amos, and Malachi.
20. Malachi 3:10.
21. Doctrine and Covenants 85:3.
22. 2 Timothy 3:12.
23. See Doctrine and Covenants 86:8–11.
24. Doctrine and Covenants 107:18.
25. See Doctrine and Covenants 132:47, 59.
26. See Abraham 2:11.
27. Isaiah 49:25; see also Doctrine and Covenants 105:14.
28. Doctrine and Covenants 98:37.
29. Thomas S. Monson, "Be of Good Cheer," *Ensign*, May 2009, 92.

Chapter 11: We Can Make Righteous Choices

1. Acts 3:25; see also 1 Nephi 15:18; 3 Nephi 20:25.
2. See "True to the Faith," *Hymns* (1985), no. 254, text by Evan Stephens.
3. "Know This, That Every Soul Is Free," *Hymns*, no. 240.
4. Doctrine and Covenants 93:36.
5. Doctrine and Covenants 130:18–19.
6. 1 Kings 10:24.
7. See 2 Nephi 2:27.
8. Doctrine and Covenants 4:6.
9. See Moses 1:39.
10. Doctrine and Covenants 14:7.
11. See Doctrine and Covenants 132:19.
12. 1 Timothy 4:12; see also Hebrews 13:7. The Greek word *anastrophe* from which *conversation* was translated means "upward manner of living."
13. Ardeth Greene Kapp, *I Walk by Faith* (1987), 87.

14. 2 Nephi 2:27.
15. Alma 41:10.
16. See 2 Nephi 10:23.
17. John 17:3.
18. Joseph Smith Translation, Matthew 6:38.
19. See Moses 1:39; Doctrine and Covenants 14:7.
20. See Doctrine and Covenants 1:16; 89:4.
21. See 1 Timothy 6:5–6, 11.
22. See Boyd K. Packer, "Counsel to Youth," *Ensign,* November 2011, 18.
23. Doctrine and Covenants 38:13.
24. Doctrine and Covenants 38:28.
25. 2 Peter 2:18–19.
26. Dr. Patrick Fagan, a senior fellow at the Family Research Council, directs the Marriage and Religion Research Institute in Washington, D.C.
27. Patrick Fagan, "The Family GDP: How Marriage and Fertility Drive the Economy," *The Family in America,* Volume 24, number 2 (Spring 2010), 136.
28. Fagan, "Family GDP," 142.
29. 2 Nephi 9:41.
30. See Doctrine and Covenants 84:88.
31. See 2 Nephi 9:51; 2 Nephi 32:3.
32. See 2 Nephi 4:34; 28:31.
33. See Doctrine and Covenants 131:1–3.
34. Doctrine and Covenants 86:8–11; emphasis added.

Chapter 12: We Can Make the Sabbath a Delight

1. Isaiah 58:13.
2. Mark 2:27.
3. See Genesis 2:2–3.
4. Exodus 20:8; see also Deuteronomy 5:12; Mosiah 13:16; 18:23.
5. See Deuteronomy 5:14–15. People who choose to work seven days a week are essentially in bondage—to work or perhaps to money, but they are slaves nevertheless. A millionaire who works seven days a week is a rich slave.
6. See Exodus 31:13, 16.
7. See Doctrine and Covenants 59:12. Prior to His Crucifixion, the Lord introduced the sacrament among His disciples at the Feast of the Passover (see Matthew 26:26–28; Mark 14:22–24). The resurrected Lord instituted the sacrament in remembrance of His Atonement among the people of ancient America (see 3 Nephi 18:1–12; Moroni 4:1–3; 5:2) and restored it in modern times (see Doctrine and Covenants 20:77, 79). Partaking of the sacrament renews our covenant made at baptism to keep His commandments (see Doctrine and Covenants 20:68).

8. See Doctrine and Covenants 20:37, 77.
9. See Matthew 12:8; Mark 2:28; Luke 6:5.
10. See Exodus 31:13; Leviticus 19:3, 30; 26:2; Doctrine and Covenants 68:29.
11. See Ezekiel 20:20; 44:24.
12. See Exodus 31:13; Ezekiel 20:12, 20.
13. Doctrine and Covenants 59:9–10, 13, 15–16.
14. See Leviticus 26:2–4.
15. See Doctrine and Covenants 128:15–18.
16. Doctrine and Covenants 88:77–78.
17. See Isaiah 61:1; Doctrine and Covenants 128:22; 138:57–59.
18. See Matthew 25:35–40.
19. Isaiah 58:13–14; emphasis added.
20. See Mosiah 2:21.
21. See 1 Timothy 4:12.

Conclusion: The World Needs Our Contribution

1. "Behold! A Royal Army," *Hymns* (1985), no. 251; text by Fanny J. Crosby.
2. See Revelation 12:7–9; Doctrine and Covenants 29:40–41.
3. See 1 Nephi 10:4.
4. 2 Nephi 2:25.
5. Unfortunately, evil is not always easily discerned. We hear of wolves dressed in sheep's clothing, suggesting that camouflage and masquerade often make true identification of the adversary's minions a bit blurry.
6. Clayton Christensen, "A theistic balance on the court," *Washington Post*, May 18, 2010.
7. Ether 2:7; emphasis added.
8. Doctrine and Covenants 1:16.
9. 2 Timothy 3:1–5.
10. 2 Timothy 3:15.
11. See Ephesians 6:13–18.
12. Doctrine and Covenants 101:3–5.
13. 2 Chronicles 32:7.
14. Isaiah 41:10.
15. 1 Corinthians 2:9.

INDEX